Putting You

June 29, 1998

Rick & Beth

May you never
need the advice in this
book.

Putting Your Heart Online

Nancy Capulet

Variable Symbols, Inc.
Oakland, California

Putting Your Heart Online
Cover and illustrations: *Ramón A. León*

Library of Congress Cataloging-in-Publication Data

Capulet, Nancy
    Putting Your Heart Online

    Includes index.
    1. Relationships 2. Self-help 3. Computer Technology

ISBN 0-9663774-0-0 *Putting Your Heart Online*
ISBN 0-9663774-1-9 *Putting Your Heart Online:*
                               Matchmaker Edition

Copyright © 1998 by Variable Symbols, Inc.

Variable Symbols, Inc.
33 Linda Avenue, Suite 2210
Oakland, CA 94611-4819
E-mail: info@HeartsOnline.com
URL: www.HeartsOnline.com

Printed in the United States of America.

10   9   8   7   6   5   4   3   2   1

To David,
for responding to my ad
and deciding that I was worth
pursuing through cyberspace.

Foreword

By following Nancy Capulet's simple recipe, you will not, overnight,

- Lose twenty pounds

- Discover the cure for male pattern baldness

- Win the Nobel Peace Price

- Be nominated for Attorney General

Nope, all of these phenomenal events won't take place thanks to your adopting the wisdom in this book. But you'll greatly improve your odds of turning those hours at the modem into a most flavorful romance.

Cliff Stoll
Author, *The Cuckoo's Egg* and *Silicon Snake Oil*
Oakland, California

Preface

"Fertile ground for the seeds of love." That's how *The New York Times*[1] describes the Internet. Want to find a mate? Look in cyberspace. You'll learn the advantages of dating online, and how to use the Net to find romance, with this friendly and informative book. It tells you how to

- Find the best Web sites
- Create a compelling and effective ad
- Search for the partner of your dreams
- Dodge cyberheads, Web weenies, and online liars
- Reduce the chaff without losing the wheat
- Flirt over your modem
- Avoid first-date fiascoes
- Turn a promising connection into a real relationship

A rapidly growing number of people are finding love online. The potential grows even greater as the number of Internet users increases daily. As of January 1998, there were approximately 102 million Internet users.[2]

Other books about dating don't include information on where to find online matchmaking services, how to select one, what to write in an online ad, or how to move safely from online communication to a face-to-face meeting. *Putting Your Heart Online* does. It's the book I wish I could have read before I posted my first online ad.

This book is largely oriented toward heterosexual relationships, but much of the material should be equally useful to gay men, lesbians, and bisexuals.

---

[1] *Seeking Fine Mind/Body. Dog Lovers a Plus.* The New York Times (February 11, 1996, page E7)

[2] Matrix Information and Directory Services, `www.mids.org`.

This book will help if you're unsure about trying romance Internet style. It includes motivational stories, exercises to get you started, and phrases to use in ads and e-mail correspondence. With straightforward guidelines, helpful hints, anecdotes, and sample templates, the book will build your self-confidence by developing your online dating skills. It includes true stories of men and women who have met their sweethearts through online matchmaking services. I based the content on hundreds of interviews, on workshops, on research, and on my own personal experience.

Organization

The book is divided into three parts. The first part introduces you to online matchmaking services, showing how they work and how to write a compelling ad. The second part focuses on finding and communicating with other singles. Section three offers ways to gather information, reject people politely, and handle rejection. The book concludes with tips that will help to move a promising relationship from the Net to the real world. The Appendix contains basic instructions to get you on the Internet and the Web, to locate sites where one can meet promising people, and suggests techniques for keeping track of new contracts. I also included a comprehensive glossary and an annotated bibliography.

Your Stories

I sincerely hope my guide helps you to find a romantic relationship. I have tried to anticipate your questions and concerns. Please let me know if I have missed something. I would also be interested in hearing about your experiences putting your heart online. I welcome all comments. I look forward to hearing from you.

Nancy Capulet
Variable Symbols, Inc.
33 Linda Avenue, Suite 2210
Oakland, CA 94611-4819
E-mail: nancy@HeartsOnline.com
URL: www.HeartsOnline.com

About Me

Putting Your Heart Online grew out of my experience as a single woman. After ending a long relationship a few years ago, I found that pursuing the usual sources—friends-of-friends, blind dates, the bar scene, parties, professional associations, print ads, dating services, and singles events did not yield a man who could be a permanent, committed part of my life. I went out on countless dates and met some interesting and attractive men, but more often I spent time and money only to discover that we weren't right for one another.

My single friends didn't realize that the exploding popularity of the World Wide Web and the Internet has made it worthwhile to look online for a partner. To me, it seemed a natural step, based on my familiarity with computers. I was amazed by the response that I received.

As I looked for my lifetime partner, I told my friends about my successes and encouraged them to get online too. Some did and were not successful. But many of them met articulate, professional, attractive, sociable people on the Net. Our social lives blossomed. I was confident I would eventually meet the man who would be right for me.

From time to time, I would meet someone with whom I thought there was potential, only to have our relationship fizzle after several months. Usually, just after a relationship ended, I'd feel jaded, but I would pull myself together and write a completely new profile. I wrote the following ad considering that men tend to be concerned about appearance.

> Intelligent (can make complete run-on sentences),
> educated (with some extra degrees), and
> attractive (big brown eyes, friendly smile,
> in great shape--bicycling and playing squash
> racquets may have something to do with
> that). So, what am I looking for? Someone
> with a similar set of qualities, who understands
> and expresses his emotions, who is adventurous,
> attractive (both inside and out), to whom
> romance and passion are not unfamiliar
> terms, and who enjoys an active life. I
> expect it may take me a while to find the
> love of my life. My search goes on ....

About a week after I placed the ad, I got e-mail from David. In my response, I sent my telephone number and asked for his. He e-mailed it and said he would call the next day. I didn't feel like waiting, so I called him that evening. We arranged to meet later that week. It wasn't love at first sight, but I had a pleasant time and I found David interesting. So when I was about to depart and he asked whether I wanted to meet for dinner the following week, I accepted.

Over the next couple of months, we saw each other quite a bit. We went out to dinner, bicycled into the hills, and spoke on the telephone nearly every evening. We were open and honest with each other. David was smitten. I enjoyed his company but thought there might be someone better for me. I let David know that. I encouraged him to meet other women and I continued to look for the man of my dreams. However, when I met other men, I was disappointed. They weren't as kind, as considerate, or as interested in me as David was.

After several months of pursuing me, David finally decided to check out other women and responded to a few online ads.

After he met Judy, he told me he was interested in seeing her again. I became worried that she might find David a great catch. That's when I realized that I cared about him more than I had previously admitted to myself.

I asked David if he was willing to give our relationship another chance. Fortunately, he was. He thought it would be a good idea if I met his parents, sisters, and brother, so he invited me to Maryland over the New Year. It was during that trip that I realized how lucky I was to have such a warm, generous, intelligent man in my life. With each passing day, it seems more and more certain that ours will be a long-term relationship. I'm incredibly glad I put my heart online.

I am not employed by any online matchmaking service. I am a computer professional. Nancy Capulet is my pseudonym. I selected the last name William Shakespeare chose for Juliet. I wonder whether Juliet's story might have had a happy ending had she and Romeo communicated via e-mail.

Acknowledgments

There are many people I wish to thank. Megan Smith encouraged me to give a talk about online dating—it was the response that I received from that presentation that provided the impetus for me to write this book. Suzie Hunter contributed to Chapter 1. Jay Cornell improved Chapters 4 and 5. David Sals, the co-founder of Romantic Partner, enriched Chapters 1, 2, and 3 and made suggestions about the overall organization. Hamish Reid came up with the title of this book. Ramón A. León designed the cover and illustrations. Lyn Dupré and Charles Egan copy edited the manuscript. My mother and father, Anne and Nelson, supported and encouraged me, and made suggestions. And many people generously allowed me to interview them.

This book is based on notes that were initially prepared for the first talk I gave on *How to Find a Mate Online.* I have revised it for subsequent workshops and presentations by incorporating the valuable comments and suggestions from many people to whom I am grateful. They include Karen Anderson, Ron Avitzur, Doug Barnes, Lori Beraha, Joel Biatch, Carole Bidnick, Susan Blachman, Bill Burnett, Grace Campbell, Henry Cejtin, Candis Condo, Mike Cowlishaw, George Csicsery, Ron Davidson, Brian Davis, Roland Dreier, Bird Emrick, Dean Esmay, Ari Davidow, Michael Fasman, Jonathan Feinstein, Jan Fire, Peter Gavin, Lise Getoor, John Glenn, Anita Goldstein, Andrew Gottlieb, Susan Graves, Leora Gregory, Ed Haas, Carrie Heeter, Craig A. Harrison, Jerry Jermann, Mary Lou Jepsen, Leslie Johnston, Sarah Keller, Rose Kemps, Bruce Koball, Gary Kremen, Howard Lakin, Mark Laubach, Eleanore Lee, Debbie Lefkowitz, Tom Lehmann, Virginia Logan, Mark Lotter, Kathleen McCleary, Trish McDermott, Elizabeth J. Mitchell, Eugene Miya, Pamela Noensie, Ellen Nold, Frank Olkin, David Oster, Eleanor Strum Oster, Karin Payson, Kent Peacock, Michael Perry, Jim Propp, John Quarterman, Elaine Richards, Eric Riess, Rick Ross, Paul Rubin, Carol Scheftic, Stephanie Schus, Will Scoggin, Nikki Smith, Shari Steele, Chuck Stevenson, Jonathan Stigelman, Linda Taylor, Tom Wadlow, Beth Weinstein, Renice Wernette, Brian Zisk, and members of the Brain Exchange. I thank Cliff Stoll and Tom Wadlow for encouraging me to persevere, and Stephanie Schus, Bruce Webster, and Cliff Stoll for telling agents and publishers about this book. I thank Robbie Hare, my agent, for believing in me, pushing me, and offering wonderful suggestions.

Nancy Capulet
San Francisco, California
May 1998

Contents

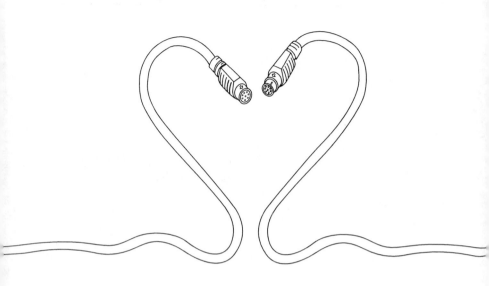

Part I

Dating on the Internet

Myth: If it's meant to be, it will happen.

What would you think if someone said, "If I'm meant to get a raise, I'll get it," "If I'm meant to win a marathon, I will," or "If I'm meant to be president of the United States, I'll be elected"? Most people have to work to achieve their goals. Why should dating be any different?

Chapter 1

Dating Online

Bob is still searching for a soulmate in bars. Carol has kissed many a frog she met on blind dates, but has never found a prince. Ted has tried cooking, hiking and stilt-walking-for-singles, without finding a partner. Alice waits at home for fate (or Aunt Minnie) to send Mr. Right. I consulted the Internet and met David, the man I'm marrying.

The exploding popularity of the Internet makes it a great tool for meeting people—especially singles! Web-based matchmaking services provide an easy-to-use and inexpensive environment that lets you communicate while maintaining your anonymity for as long as you choose. By exchanging e-mail, you can converse with many people and increase your odds of finding the right match; it's easy to weed out those people with whom you feel incompatible or uncomfortable. And you get to know people who seem promising before meeting them in person.

People Who Should Read This Book

Anyone who can use a computer; anyone who wants to develop new friendships, have an exciting social life, or meet the "right" person for a lasting relationship. Online dating provides a way for shy people to venture out of their shells and still feel safe. On the Internet, adventurous seekers can meet other interested, compatible singles quickly and conveniently. Online services make it easy to search by age, interests, location, religion, ethnicity—and thus can serve practically everyone.

Success Stories

People have different goals for going online. In these stories, success is defined by happiness. All of the stories in this book are based on people's real-life experiences online.

Rosanne hadn't had much luck dating people in her industry. At a party, she heard about an online matchmaking service, but because she had had a bad experience as the result of a personal ad in a newspaper, Rosanne was apprehensive. Still, since she didn't want to go to bars and she wasn't being invited to many places where there were single men, she decided to put her heart online. She was soon glad that she had. She received lots of responses and filled her free time meeting the men who sounded interesting. The scope of the Net was broad, so she even arranged meetings while she was on business trips. Within six weeks of joining the matchmaking service, she met Josh. Within five months of their first e-mail message, he moved in to her apartment. About six months later, they bought a condo; now they are living happily together. They both are divorced, so they would rather not get married—at least not yet.

Paul who is sixty-three and retired. He joined an online service and asked for women in the Chicago area who wanted to meet a man his age, and he found several likely candidates. He's having a great time flying to different parts of the world with his friends. The last time I talked to him, he was taking a trip to New Zealand with Brenda, whom he met online.

Florence's husband died unexpectedly. A woman in Florence's office described her experiences running a newspaper personal ad, which got Florence thinking about what she would say if she were to place an ad. Around that time, Florence was surfing the Internet and found an online matchmaking service. Just for fun, she placed an ad. Because she's five feet, ten inches, and 240 lbs, Florence figured she might have to contact lots of men to find a partner. Much to her surprise, scores of men wrote to her and seemed genuinely interested in her. It took only a few months before she met Mark, whom she later married. You can find Mark's ad on page 46.

Andrew, the only reporter for a small-town Wisconsin newspaper, is another matchmaking success. As a single father, he wanted to meet women who had children about the same age as his daughter, Stephanie. Through the Internet he met Laurie, a divorcée in the same county whose two children were within a year of Stephanie's age. When Andrew and Laurie finally met, after a month of e-mail correspondence, they hit it off immediately. They're now married, a happy family with three children.

Diana's story is a little different. She is an only child and attended a women's college. She felt uncomfortable around men. After posting her ad online, she received scores of responses and went out with the senders of about a dozen of them. Although none seemed right to her, the experience made her more comfortable and confident about dating. Her new self-confidence was obvious and she got more invitations from men in the course of her daily affairs. Now she's going out with Ken, whom she met at a friend's dinner party.

Margie is a U.S. Army emergency-room physician who works the night shift and sleeps during the day. She's always been a night person, so this reverse schedule doesn't bother her. She wanted to meet someone who also works nights. Using online dating services, she has met two men who fit into her nocturnal schedule. One works for a morning newspaper and keeps hours similar to hers; another, an artist, likes to paint at night. At the moment, she's checking them both out.

An appealing aspect of online dating is that you're not limited to people who live in your area. Kathy, formerly an art-history professor at a junior college, found Franco, an Italian mechanical engineer residing in Milan. Without the Internet, they never would have met. Kathy didn't speak Italian then and certainly wouldn't have read personal ads in Italian newspapers. But Franco, who learned English as a child, ended up in cyberspace on the same online dating service as Kathy. Their criteria matched; they began corresponding, and they had an intense written romance. As a Christmas present, Franco sent Kathy an airline ticket to Rome. Shortly after that trip, they got married; Kathy is now living in Milan.

These people are not unusual. Online personal ads have helped many to lead happier, more interesting lives.

Frequently Asked Questions

When I speak to professional groups about online dating, I'm asked the following questions:

- How does it work?
- Will I meet people I'll like?
- What about chemistry?
- What about the ratio of men to women?
- Is it safe?

Here are my answers.

How Does Online Dating Work?

There are numerous ways to find dates online. Online matchmaking services and personal ad sites each have two components: the World Wide Web and e-mail.

♡♡♡

Here is some background information for people who
have little knowledge of or experience with the Internet. The *World Wide Web*, also known as the *Web*,
is a collection of information stored on different computers around the world.

Get on a computer with a Web page viewing program (called a browser), an Internet account, a modem and a telephone line or a direct connection (cable
or Ethernet). Then, connect to your Internet account,
log on, start your browser, type a Web address (such
as `http://www.HeartsOnline.com`), also known as a
URL (Universal Resource Locator), and start reading.

When you're connected, you click on highlighted
text—a *link*—and your browser gathers more information (which may be stored halfway around the
world on a different Web page). Your browser then
displays it. It is these many links that make this collection of information behave like a web.

E-mail is a message that you create on your computer and send to another computer user. When the
recipient logs in, he can read your e-mail and reply
to it. E-mail's main advantage is that it's usually accessible to the recipient within seconds—but, unlike
a telephone call, it doesn't require that both parties
be available at the same time. People who communicate via e-mail don't have to play telephone tag.
For more information on the Internet and the World
Wide Web, see Appendix A.

Most online dating services work in basically the same way.
After logging into the site, you are asked for your name and

e-mail address. This information goes into a database but cannot be seen by any other members.

Many dating sites charge a small membership fee, generally around $10 per month. It's a good idea and worth the cost—joining requires you to complete an application form and use a credit card, thus discouraging pranksters who might otherwise abuse the system. Some sites offer free trials.

Most sites ask you to select a *handle*, or screen name, and a password. You'll use both each time you log on. Handles vary depending on the system you're using. Some sites encourage you to use your first name; others let you pick any word or sequence of characters. Here are examples of handles:

```
Balthazar34    Mary_Louise        SweetNSpicy
Bermuda_Girl   outdoorsy          Tall_Romeo
Da_One_4U      new2SF             theCook
Fervent        SixFoot2EyesBlue   zzzz
```

Then you provide information to create a *profile*: a description of yourself and your interests. You are asked about characteristics such as age, ethnicity, religion, smoking and drinking habits, marital status, educational level, as well as one or more essay questions about your lifestyle, interests, and the kind of person you are seeking. The service might also offer you the opportunity to include one or more photographs, a voice recording, or a video clip.

Your profile is then made available to other members of the service. If they like what they see, they can send e-mail to your handle.

Profiles often are put into categories such as "Women Seeking Men" or "Men Seeking Women." Members browse the ads as they would the newspaper classifieds section. (These sites are often called *Online Classifieds*.)

Many sites go further and ask you, often through multiple-choice questions, to describe the person whom you are seeking.

You are able to specify the age, height, and lifestyle of your ideal match. The system then uses your answers to search through the profile databases to find members who meet your criteria. Sites that use such a system are known as *Online Dating Services*.

Some sites offer more sophisticated searching tools for finding compatible members that take into account both your preferences and those of the people you are considering. For example, even if you meet all of Sam's requirements, if he doesn't meet yours (suppose you want a man in his thirties and Sam is fifty-five), you aren't considered compatible. Sites that provide *two-way matching* are *Online Matchmaking Services*. These services still don't connect you with compatible members. It's up to you to review profiles and to decide what steps you want to take.

Whatever the system, once you find a profile that you like, you use the service to send an e-mail message to the author using his handle. The service redirects this e-mail to the member's account. Your e-mail shows only your handle (e.g., `Fervent`) and hides your real e-mail address (e.g., `nancy@HeartsOnline.com`).

The person who receives your message can log onto the service and access your profile using your handle. He won't be told your real name, address (e-mail or snail mail[1]), or telephone number, but he can reply to your e-mail message. If and when the time is right, you can arrange telephone calls and in-person meetings.

Will I Meet People I'll Like?

Who uses online personal ads? Men and women

- Who have access to computers
- Who are from all walks of life, of varying ages, interests, and objectives

---

[1]Snail mail is online jargon for physical or postal mail, as opposed to electronic or computer mail.

- Who are interested in connecting with other people
- Who are busy and don't always have the time or desire to meet other people at bars, at singles events, or through old-style dating services
- Who are willing to try a relatively new tool

The Internet allows you to reach these people. With computer dating, you describe yourself and the types of people whom you seek. The service uses the information to find possible candidates. For example, you can browse the profiles of people who live within forty miles of your house, are in their thirties, are Christian, and are interested in marriage and children.

There's a common misconception that only "losers" would need to use a dating service. In fact, people from all walks of life use them. Many people just don't have time for the more traditional dating methods. Some don't fit in with the singles scene. Other people are too shy to approach strangers. And even people who are comfortable at singles events may not meet the people they seek.

What About Chemistry?

Skeptics often ask me: "Even if I correspond online with someone who seems interesting, how do I know there will be chemistry when we meet in person?"

When people say "chemistry," they are in part referring to looks, which is an easy problem to solve. Many online dating services encourage members to display their photographs. It's a good idea because, as you'll see on page 56, personal ads with photos tend to get more responses than ads containing only text. You can also attach photographic images to e-mail. (See Appendix A on page 169 for instructions on this).

Looks aren't everything, however. Through e-mail, you can often learn a great deal about another person—likes, dislikes, hobbies, literacy, personality, quirks, and sense of humor. In her writing and in the questions she asks, a person discloses her nature—for better or for worse. You get to know someone from the inside out. Admittedly, words and photographs can't tell you whether there will be chemistry, but they can at least alert you to the possibility of its existence.

What About the Ratio of Men to Women?

For now, there are considerably more men than women using on-line matchmaking services. They have different experiences: Men have difficulty getting replies; women are deluged with e-mail.

That can be a problem, especially if you are a man who isn't outgoing. Women rarely initiate contact. So if you are waiting to hear from women, you could wait for a long time. But if you read Chapter 8, you'll learn how to improve your chances of getting responses from the women to whom you write.

Is it Safe?

Online dating is safer than picking someone up at a club or a bar, but it's not as safe as hiding in your room with the covers over your head. Commonly, your identity is protected by *anonymous e-mail*. With systems that support anonymous e-mail, a message isn't sent directly to you. Instead, it's sent to the handle you use for the dating service, and then forwarded to you electronically. Here's an example of how anonymous e-mail works:

> Suppose you select the handle `CutiePie` and that your e-mail address is `jenny@heartsonline.com`. You read the ad of a man whose handle is `CrazyRedhead`. His real e-mail address is `hzoft472@aol.com`—but there's no way for you to know that. The ad appeals to you, so you decide to respond. You write a message addressed to `CrazyRedhead`, his dating-service handle.

The matchmaking service receives your note for CrazyRedhead, removes information revealing your true identity, and replaces it with your handle. It then forwards your message to CrazyRedhead, a.k.a. hzoft472@aol.com. He sees only that the message comes from CutiePie. He doesn't see your e-mail address or your real name.

The computers used by your matchmaking system know the real e-mail address for CutiePie and the real e-mail address for CrazyRedhead. Because they send the mail indirectly, your anonymity is preserved— until, if ever, you choose to reveal your identity.

I often think of my friend, Jenny, when I'm explaining the advantage of anonymous re-mailing. Jenny was hesitant to place an online ad. As a young associate with a stodgy law firm, she thought it important to separate her personal life from work. Her private life, she thought, was her own business.

Most important though, Jenny had the same justifiable fears of any way of meeting strangers—be it via online, newspaper advertisements, dating services, or chance encounters. When she decides that there's little point in pursuing a relationship, she wants to be able to break off contact quickly. Jenny saw that anonymous e-mail was an ideal solution; should CrazyRedhead indeed turn out to be crazy, all he would know would be her handle.

All dating involves taking risks and putting yourself out there, but with online dating, you have more control over what risks you take. You can correspond online with someone for months without his ever knowing your telephone number or address. You can arrange to meet someone without telling him your last name.

Drawbacks and Advantages

Of course, online dating does have drawbacks. For one thing, not everyone finds a lifetime mate—or even a casual date. You still need interpersonal skills to communicate with and to meet someone. And, just as in real life, you'll find jerks, bores, liars, and con artists on the Internet.

Some people believe that it's particularly difficult to develop a relationship with someone you've met online. Written and face to face communication are different. People develop fantasies about their online correspondents—fantasies that shatter when they actually meet. I'll deal with these issues in Chapter 9.

These are minor drawbacks to online dating, but the advantages are significant. Here's a summary of the advantages of looking for a mate online:

- *Safe* — You don't have to reveal your identity. Many systems provide anonymous e-mail. This feature will appeal to people who don't want their acquaintances to know what they are doing online.

- *Convenient* — You can access a service anytime, from any location where you have Internet access.

- *Searchable* — Millions of singles use the Internet. Fortunately, many online matchmaking services provide tools to help you identify people whom you find interesting and attractive. You can set up your own personalized profile and define key attributes you seek or offer to potential matches. The service presents you with those other users who meet your criteria (one-way matching). Some services also provide two-way matching, i.e., people who meet your criteria and you, theirs. You choose whom to contact and whom to meet.

- *Lots of information* — More information is available online than in most newspaper personal ads. You can e-mail questions to find out even more about a person. Unlike print personal ads, where you're often at the mercy of the telephone, with online service the recipient can answer your questions at her convenience. Many services include photographs of members.

- *Great people* — I've found that many wonderful people place online personal ads. Often, they are interesting and successful people who lead busy lives.

- *Lots of people* — If you're like me, you anticipate having to meet and date many different people before finding the right one. Using online matchmaking services, you can get in touch with many more people than you can through your everyday activities.

- *Good value* — The cost for most online matchmaking services is reasonable. The monthly fee is usually about $10; compare that with $10 per attempt for newspaper personals, or $1000 minimum per year for matchmaking services.

Many couples who meet through the Internet say their paths simply wouldn't have crossed, had they not been looking online. They live in different locations, or they aren't involved in the same activities. Or they are too involved in their work to notice anyone in the course of their normal activities. The Internet gave them the power to reach across cyberspace and to find each other.

Chapter 2

Making Online Dating Work

Jenny, a thirty-four year-old patent attorney, now uses the Internet frequently to learn about existing patents and related works. She used to rely on friends for introductions. Then, she moved to San Francisco. After settling into her new apartment, she started looking for ways to improve her social life. Using the CupidNet Online Romance directory (URL `www.cupidnet.com`; see page 23 for other directories), she browsed several services, and logged in to one that caught her eye. She chose the handle, or screen name, `NewToArea`, after discovering that `Effervescent` was already taken.

With all the single men using this Internet service, Jenny has no shortage of candidates. Jenny can correspond electronically with guys whose profiles she likes, or with ones who respond to her ad. Sounds easy, right? Well ... maybe.

A Cautionary Tale

Men and women tend to have different experiences using online matchmaking services. Let's watch what happens to Jenny, our thirty-four year-old patent attorney, and to Jim, a thirty-six year-old San Francisco architect, in their first experiences with online dating.

September 1, Evening

Jenny gets home, turns on her computer, and logs on to the Internet. She has decided to try out a popular matchmaking site located in San Francisco and available all around the world. She signs on as a guest, which allows her to browse the ads without registering for the service. After she looks at about a dozen of them, she signs up for a free trial account and writes her profile. She quickly answers the multiple-choice questions, and then spends over an hour deciding how to describe herself. She looks at a dozen more ads, revises her profile, puts it online, and prints it out. She scans a few more profiles, prints them out, logs out, and turns off her computer and modem.

Jim grabs a burrito on his way home from a workshop on Internet dating. While he's eating it, he jots down ideas for an ad. He turns on his PC and modem and logs in to a matchmaking Web site. He browses about five ads, signs up for a free trial membership, writes his profile, and posts it. Then, he browses more ads and sends messages to eight women.

September 2, Morning

Before Jenny leaves for work, she checks her e-mail. She finds twelve new e-mail messages; four are responses to her online ad. She doesn't want to be late for work, so she decides to put off answering them.

Jim checks his e-mail. He has thirteen messages, but none from anyone on the matchmaking service. He logs in to the service, glances at more profiles, and sends e-mail to four more women.

September 2, Afternoon

Jenny checks her e-mail while she is at work. She finds seven new messages from members of the matchmaking service. She notices that more than a quarter of the men are more than ten years older than she is, even though she stated in her criteria she's interested in only men who are within five years of her age. One man offers to be her love slave. She discards the messages from men who don't interest her.

Jim also checks his e-mail from work. He finds a single response from one of the women he wrote to the previous evening. He immediately writes her a long note. He browses ads again, and writes to an additional six women. He's now written to eighteen women.

September 8 (Five Days Later)

Jenny receives her eighty-fourth response. She's written back to only eleven of them. She is corresponding with seven men and finds the task overwhelming. So as not to elicit more responses, she makes her profile invisible by checking an option box.

Jim updates his profile for the ninth time that week. He has heard back from only one of the forty-nine women to whom he has written. She sent him three e-mail messages and then stopped writing to him, with no explanation. Jim wonders why these women are placing ads on the system but are not responding to his e-mail, especially given that he meets all their matching criteria. "Something is wrong here," he thinks. "Maybe they didn't get my e-mail." Trying to stay optimistic, he sends each of them a note asking whether they received his previous e-mail.

September 9

Jim receives six e-mail messages, all in a similar vein. Yes, women have received his e-mail but they are inundated with responses to their ads. They write back just to be polite.

September 23 (Two Weeks Later)

Jenny has now met eight of her online suitors. None has caught her fancy, so she puts her profile back online and writes to four men whose profiles she finds enticing.

For the past week, Jim has been corresponding with two women. One, to whom he wrote on his first day using the service, waited a week to respond. He receives a message, out of the blue, from `NewToArea` (which we know—but Jim doesn't—is Jenny's handle). He wonders what is wrong with her that she has to seek out men instead of having them pursue her. Cautiously, he writes back.

The Vicious Cycle

The online dating environment can create a vicious cycle. Men don't hear back from the women they approach, so they write to more women; the women are bombarded with responses, and therefore ignore most of them.

Should Jim feel discouraged that fifty-four women never even acknowledged his e-mail? Why aren't they writing back? Some are just not interested. Others are out of town. But, like Jenny, most are simply overwhelmed.

Both Jenny's and Jim's experiences are typical. Few women initiate contact. Men are usually the pursuers, scanning women's ads and writing to the ones that they select. Men write to lots of women, most of whom don't respond. Women say they get buried under all the responses they receive.

What's Going On?

Imagine you're a single man at a party where there are 100 people: ninety-five men and five women. All the men are single; all are interested in meeting women. A few men approach every female present; others have enjoyable conversations with several women; the rest wait for women to approach them. This situation isn't good for the men, because their chances of success are low. Most of the women, on the other hand, feel bothered by all the attention.

Fortunately, the Internet ratio of men to women isn't so lopsided: it's about three to one. But there are factors that pose additional problems to both men and women looking for mates.

Men in their forties and fifties who want to father children prefer to date women under thirty-five. Many women under thirty-five want men around their own age. In general, short men will go out with shorter or taller women, but tall women want taller men, and short women also want tall men. Few people want overweight mates—even those who are themselves overweight. Many people are willing to reject a candidate based on little information.

Jim can't look into a given woman's eyes and see whether she is interested in him, and he can't see how many other men are also pursuing her. Often, because women are hesitant to put their photographs on the web, Jim can't even tell whether he might find a woman physically attractive. He decides that he might as well write to dozens to improve his chances of meeting just one.

Jenny, on the other hand, studies the responses she receives and attempts to determine which ones are worth following up. What she might be able to tell at a glance at a party can take hours of investigation and e-mail correspondence online. However, through the service's profiles, she does find out things, such as a man's interest in having children, marital status, or drinking habits, that she might not feel comfortable asking about when she would first meet someone.

Beating the Cycle

So how do you deal with the gender imbalance? How do you take advantage of your situation and get more responses from people you consider desirable?

- Be honest. What good will it do you if she falls for an imaginary six-foot-tall man, only to find that the real you is five feet, seven inches? How do you expect him to react when he finds out you're not thirty-five—you're forty-two? Good, lasting relationships are built on a foundation of honesty.

- In your ad and in your e-mail, show your personality, interests, and passions, so like-minded people can find you and have topics to talk about when they respond.

- Choose a handle that presents a positive, memorable image. You can use your handle to tell people something about yourself or to start a conversation.

- If you're comfortable doing so, include a photograph in your profile—most services provide the option. Many people do consider appearance in choosing a date. People who are attracted to your image will write with increased enthusiasm; those who aren't, won't write. It will save you the disappointment of their reactions to seeing you.

- Just as a job seeker tailors his cover letter to match each company he contacts, tailor the responses you send. Describe what caught your interest. For further tips on how to respond to an ad, see Chapter 8.

- If you don't get responses to your ad and e-mail message, consider revising them. Ask your friends for suggestions, and see Chapter 5.

- Have fun! When you are relaxed and are having fun, it shows—and it's attractive.

Tips for Women

- Be honest about your looks and body type. If you're slender, say so. If you're overweight, admit it.

- Describe what you want; your words may cause some people to lose interest, but those who respond are more likely to suit your tastes.

- When someone writes to you, be considerate and let him know that you received his message. For example, you could say something like this:

      Thanks for writing to me. I received your
      message. I'll check out your profile.

  Such notes will help you to avoid having to wade through "Did you get my last e-mail?" messages.

- Write back promptly, even if just to say "I'll write more later." Keep the momentum going. For guidelines on e-mail good etiquette, see Chapter 7.

Tips for Men

- Don't expect women to write to you first, based on your ad. Although they sometimes will, more often you'll have to catch their attention. Write a personal message that refers to something in her profile. At this stage, your goal is to start a conversation. For recommendations on how to elicit responses, see Chapter 8.

- Post a profile, even if you initiate all conversations and include your ad in your e-mail. Otherwise, you are not fully participating, and some women may consider you a stalker.

- Don't be put off if a woman does initiate contact. More and more women who are tired of being approached in clubs, bars, and on the street are using the Internet to take a more active approach in selecting people to date.

- Pay attention to the women's criteria. If she says that she wants to meet someone between thirty and thirty-five, and you're forty, say so up front, then explain why she might be interested in you anyway.

- Carefully consider your e-mail subject lines. First impressions usually last, and your subject line is your chance to make a great first impression. Remember that you may be competing with twenty other pieces of mail. Here are examples of subject lines:

  - Want to go sailing?
  - Let's dance the night away (preferably in Latin style)
  - I'm not a fan of makeup either

- Hang in there, even if you receive no responses. If a woman interests you and you don't hear back from her for a couple of weeks, send her another e-mail message. Many women who advertise online are meeting men. Eventually, one of them will want to meet you. Perseverance pays off.

Chapter 3

Choosing a Service

Currently, there are hundreds of sites offering relationship services and the number keeps growing. Each matchmaking service has its own personality.

How do you find matchmaking sites? Friends, your dates, and other people on the Internet may be able to provide you with referrals. There are many great directories of matchmaking sites, including:

- Cupid's Network (`www.cupidnet.com`)
- Hearts Online (`www.HeartsOnline.com`)
- SinglesSites (`www.singlesites.com`)
- Yahoo! (`www.yahoo.com`).
- Safedate (`www.safedate.org`)

The last is a directory service that provides reviews and rates sites according to their safety, indicating, among other information, whether a site offers anonymous e-mail and e-mail verification. Ethnic and religious Web sites sometimes point to services for singles interested in locating people of the same ethnicity or religion.

Look for sites that win recognition and awards, such as:

- Lycos' Top 5 % of the web (`www.pointcom.com`)

- Magellan's 4-star site (www.mckinley.com)
- PC Magazine's Top 100 Web sites (www.zdnet.com)

Sites often list their awards on their home page. See which sites are described in the newspaper, advertised on the radio, or mentioned on other Web pages. Sites that market themselves are more likely to have a large pool of members.

You can use a *search engine* to find matchmaking sites by searching for words such as *dating, matchmaking* or *matchmakers, personals, romance*, and *singles*. A search engine looks for information on the Internet. A list of popular search engines is included in Appendix B on page 175.

What to Consider

How do you choose from among the ever-increasing number of online matchmaking sites? Which online matchmaking service is best suited for your needs? This chapter focuses on how to select a site. Appendix F mentions particular sites.

Consider the membership, the information included in a profile, the features and services, and the cost.

Membership

A dating service is only as good as its members. Before spending time developing your personal ad, check who is using the site.

- *Number of interesting people* — How many active members on the service are of interest to you? Run a search and see.

- *Demographics* — What is the ratio of men to women on the site? What are the ages of the members? It may not be easy to find such information. You could, for example, search for the number of women and the number of men between the ages of 25 and 30, 30 and 35, 35 and 40, and compare the numbers that you obtain.

- *Region* — Where do most of the members live? Finding a site with members in your area increases your chances of meeting someone who lives nearby. Run searches to find how many members live in geographically desirable locations.

- *Special interest* — Why was the site established? Read the site's home page to see what it says about the approach. Is the site intended for people of your age, religion, and background? Does it promote any particular activities or lifestyle?

- *Statistics* — What statistics are available to members on the site? Some sites provide little or no statistics about other members; others indicate when members signed up, when they most recently used the service, how many people have contacted each member, and how many messages a person has sent. Do you consider their statistics helpful or intrusive?

Profile

Quite a bit can be learned from a person's profile; how much varies from service to service.

- *Detail* — Is there enough information available about each person for you to make reasonable choices? Are you overwhelmed by a sea of too much text?

- *Types of questions* — What types of questions are asked: multiple choice or essay? Do you choose from preset lists? Are you given space to answer questions in your own personal way? Will the answers to the questions help you in selecting dates?

- *Presentation* — Is the information presented in an easy-to-read format?

- *Media* — Can you include photographs with your profile? If so, how many? What about voice recordings or video clips?

- *Time requirements* — How long does it take for you to create a profile? Do you consider it a worthwhile investment of your time? How do you think other people will react to filling out the forms? If the questionnaire is long, it may scare away potential members. On the other hand, people who do take the time to fill out a long form have a substantial investment in the service and may commit to using it.

Features

Online dating services provide tools for sorting through profiles and communicating.

- *Browsing* — How do you find other members who meet your desires? What criteria does the service use to determine whom to present to you? What criteria can be used for searching (for example, age, sexual preferences, ethnicity, education, distance, telephone area code, religion, height, weight, marital status)? Some systems compute the distance to other members based on their zip codes. Others let you search based on telephone area codes, which is less specific. Can you search for a specific word or phrase, like "ski"? Does the system allow you to browse ads with photographs?

- *Matching system* — Does your profile include criteria that you want in the person you hope to meet? Are you able to find members who meet your criteria and you theirs (two-way matches)? Do you have to match exactly, or does the system present you with users who are close to what you request?

- *Blocking* — Most dating-service members are polite and well behaved. To give you a way to deal with the occasional oddball or overly persistent member, some services allow you to block specific members from viewing your profile and/or contacting you. Some also allow you to block ads that you have seen and would rather not see again.

- *Hot list* — The hot-list function allows you to keep track of people whom you find interesting. You can also use it to keep track of people to whom you've sent e-mail.

- *Featured profiles* — Some sites feature profiles that they recommend you check out, which may encourage people to write better profiles.

- *Automated agent* — Does the system notify you automatically when a person who matches your criteria signs up for the service? For more on automated agents, see page 81.

- *E-mail verification* — Some systems verify your e-mail address by sending you a message to which you reply, or you log in to their service using information they provided in their e-mail message to you. This authentication verifies that your e-mail address is what you claim it to be; it protects against someone impersonating you.

- *Anonymous e-mail* — How do you contact other members? Most services allow you to send and receive anonymous e-mail using a handle or alias. Do you prefer to have your e-mail forwarded to your regular e-mail account, or would you rather log onto the matchmaking site to read your messages? If your messages are forwarded, they will be mixed in with your other e-mail. Services that retain your e-mail sometimes provide capabilities to assist you in organizing your messages. Some people find it time consuming and inconvenient to log into a site to check for messages. Other

people may have only business e-mail and may not want
dating service messages showing up there. (You may be
able to set up a free e-mail account just for your online
dating correspondence using a free e-mail provider like Hotmail, www.hotmail.com, see page 91.)

- *Chat rooms* — Chat rooms allow you to communicate in
  real time with one or more members. Chat rooms are
  like conference calls: Participants type their messages and
  the text is displayed as soon as they hit the *return* key.
  For more information on chat rooms, see page 186 of Appendix B.

- *Discussion groups* — Discussion groups function much like
  bulletin boards; users submit postings for all to read.

- *Online periodicals* — Many dating services offer an online
  newsletter or magazine with columns about psychology,
  dating trends, upcoming events, and answers to frequently
  asked questions. Online periodicals offer further insights
  into the membership of and organization behind these services.

- *Profile ordering* — Some services list the profiles of active
  members first. Other services list profiles according to how
  closely they match your criteria.

- *Activity indication* — Some services indicate the most recent date on which a member logged in to the service. This
  feature enables you to see which members are active.

Costs

Sites vary in what they charge for membership and in how they
collect their fees.

- *Free* — Many services initially offer complimentary memberships until enough people have signed up. Some sites offer free memberships with a limited set of features. Some are always free; they make their money from advertisers who place banner ads. In general, free sites attract some people who are not serious about forming relationships.

- *Trial period* — Many sites offer a free trial period that ranges from one week to several months. A trial period provides an excellent opportunity for you to test a service before you decide whether to join. After the trial period expires, the site will usually disable one or more features, and offer you a discount to entice you to join.

- *Tokens* — Most sites require payment in the form of monthly, quarterly, semi-annual or annual payments, but some sites use the token system. You purchase electronic tokens; each time that you send e-mail to another member you spend a token. The advantage of such a system is that you pay only when you communicate with a member. The disadvantage is that each e-mail costs money, so members may send long messages to get their money's worth. They may send few messages, thus reducing the chances of your connecting with someone.

Questions to Consider

Here are some questions to consider when you select a site:

- How many people are there who have characteristics I desire?
- How easy is it to find them?
- Does the service provide information that is useful?
- Do I feel comfortable providing the information requested?

- Are the questions and possible answers relevant to what my own interests are and how I like to present myself?

- Is the information presented in an easy-to-read format?

- Can I search for people who meet a particular set of criteria; for example, thirty-five to forty-five years old, live within ten miles, and are interested in having children?

- Does the service indicate which members are active? Might I end up contacting people who are no longer using the service?

- How do I contact someone whom I find interesting?

- Does the service provide anonymous e-mail, so I don't have to reveal my identity? (If not, setting up a free e-mail account for that purpose can protect your privacy. But if users expect you to identify yourself in your e-mail, they may respond less favorably to anonymous e-mail.)

- How do I receive e-mail from the service? Some people prefer to have e-mail forwarded to their e-mail account rather than picking it up at a Web page.

- Does the service provide free browsing so that I can determine whether the service suits my needs before I sign up?

- How much does the service cost?

For brief descriptions of a few sites, see Appendix F.

Hearts Online (`www.HeartsOnline.com`)

The Web is evolving and new sites crop up constantly and old sites disappear or change name. The free Hearts Online Web site, `www.HeartsOnline.com`, provides up-to-date information.

Chapter 4

Understanding Yourself

Believe it or not, many people who are looking for a mate don't know what they want. But if you don't know, how will you know when you find it? This chapter is designed to get you thinking about who you are, whom you want, and why someone would want to be with you.

State of Mind

Your state of mind has a lot to do with who will find you attractive. People are attractive when they feel good and are enjoying themselves. If you don't like yourself, then if someone likes you, you probably will think she has poor taste.

What can you do if you don't like yourself? Change. It's true that changing yourself is rarely easy. But you aren't likely to change if you don't at least try.

In 1950, my mother was thirty-one years old and still single. All her friends were already married. She hated her nose. She thought that it was getting in the way of finding a husband— and it probably was because she didn't feel good about herself. So she had a nose job. She also had a perm and bought new clothes. Shortly thereafter, she met the man who became her husband, and my father. Ironically, my father couldn't tell that my mother had had a nose job; he's legally blind. So it wasn't the cosmetic surgery, the perm, or her new clothes that attracted my father. But those things increased my mother's self-esteem and, thus, made her more desirable to my father, and probably to other men.

What's important is not that my mother changed, but that she did *something*. People who sit around feeling sorry for themselves are more likely to remain alone. People who take the initiative are most likely get where they want to be. Initiative itself is attractive. Furthermore, initiative leads you in a positive direction, even if it doesn't immediately lead to a mate.

Certain things you can't change—your age, your height, and your family. But your self-esteem is under your control. Love yourself unconditionally. That means love yourself regardless of your IQ, your wardrobe, your job, or your looks.

Many people don't have a high enough opinion of themselves. I had that problem. I used to feel unhappy that I had not achieved more. I thought that I had fallen short of my ambitions. I didn't have a doctoral degree. I wasn't climbing up the corporate ladder as fast as some of my colleagues. Stacy, a good friend, told me something that changed my view. "If you compare yourself to Mozart in music, and Einstein in physics, undoubtedly you won't think much of yourself. However, could Mozart or Einstein live your life? No. You are the best person at being you. No one can do that better than you." Now I don't compare myself with other people. I get inspiration from them, but I lead my own life—and I'm happy with it.

Are you down on yourself? Are you pessimistic about your future? Stop thinking negative thoughts! Imagine what your life would be like if you were exactly the person you wanted to be. What would you do? How would you act? Start doing those things. Start working on that script and playing that role. If you start acting like a gorgeous swan, people will stop treating you like an ugly duckling.

You'll never be happy with or truly love anyone until you're happy with and truly love yourself. Being happy with yourself is no guarantee that you'll meet someone, but it should help.

Exercise: Assessing Who You Are

1. How would one of your best friends describe you to a potential blind date? What makes you special? Why would someone want to spend time with you? What activities do you enjoy? What are your greatest personal and professional accomplishments? Here are candidate qualities to consider:

adventuresome	enthusiastic	organized
affectionate	flexible	outgoing
ambitious	friendly	self-assured
articulate	gentle	perceptive
athletic	good-looking	professional
cautious	happy	quiet
compassionate	healthy	smart
confident	honest	studious
creative	imaginative	successful
dependable	independent	trustworthy
detail-oriented	intelligent	witty
educated	literate	worldly
efficient	loving	youthful

2. Make a list of your achievements—accomplishments of which you're proud. You won't necessarily want to detail these achievements in your ad, but making this list may help you see how to present yourself positively.

Words of Advice

Believe in yourself. Have a positive attitude. Be a great catch—if you don't think you are, take steps to change. Don't look to find the right person. Look to *be* the right person.

Whom You Want

When I was placing personal ads, I met many men who had little interest in physical exercise. I was interested in meeting someone who enjoys keeping in good physical shape. So I amended my ad: "I would like to meet a man who is in great physical shape." To my surprise—but not to my delight—most of the men who responded were in tremendous shape. They were basically jocks; they were too focused on physical exercise for my taste.

So I revised my ad. "I would like to meet a man who keeps physically active, like me." The men who responded were physically fit, but exercise wasn't the center of their lives. *What I learned from my experience was to ask for what I want; I'm more likely to get it if I do.*

How do you decide what characteristics you like? Consider that people who have similar values and goals are more likely to stay together. Consequently, introduction services often ask applicants about their lifestyles—spending habits, religion, education, social activities—so that they can match people who have similar values. What lifestyle do you currently pursue? What lifestyle would you like to pursue?

Anthony, who's five feet, six inches tall, noticed that most women say in their ads that they are looking for a man who is between five feet, ten inches and six feet, five inches. I decided to check this out by signing on as a man and counting how many women matched with me when I varied my height from five feet, six inches to six feet, eight inches. Figure 4.1 shows what I found.

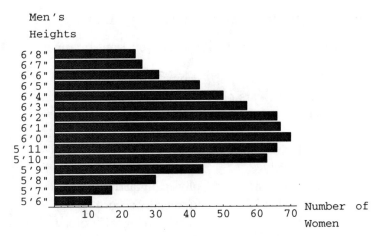

Figure 4.1: Number of women who match a man who is the height specified.

These results were consistent with Anthony's observation. When I posed as a man of five feet, six inches, I matched only one-sixth of the number of women who I matched when I posed as a man who is six feet tall. Women don't specify tall men because eighty-five percent of men are that tall. They do it because many of them receive more responses than they can handle, so they list a few characteristics that they find ideal. Why do they want tall men? Is it because they wear heels and don't want to be taller than their dates? Could it be because ads, movies, commercials, and magazines, show men taller and stronger than women? I just advised you to ask for what you want. But consider that, by putting a height restriction on your ad, you might cut out someone who is desirable in every other way. The moral of this story: *Put restrictions only on characteristics that are deeply important to you. Consider writing to people who don't match you on one criterion, if they are otherwise compatible.*

Exercise: Qualities You Want in a Mate

Write down at least ten qualities that you want in a mate.

honest	wants children
35 to 45 years old	physically fit
sensitive	nonsmoker
witty	gregarious
kind	humorous
educated	appreciates me
independent	physically attractive
enjoys his job	financially secure
intelligent	warm/caring/affectionate
professional	successful at work

Write an *E* next to qualities that you consider *essential*—nonnegotiable—and put a *D* next to items that you consider *desirable*, but not necessary—that you could live without. What items have caused you *problems* in your past relationships? Put an *P* by those. Here's an example:

honest E	wants children D
35 to 45 years old D	physically fit E
sensitive E	nonsmoker E
witty D	gregarious D
kind E	humorous D
educated D	appreciates me E
independent D	physically attractive D
enjoys his job D	financially secure E
intelligent E	warm/caring/affectionate E
professional D	successful at work P

While making your list, keep in mind a few things:

- Make sure that your desires are yours, rather than those of your parents, friends, or society.

- For each essential quality, try imagining someone who falls short on that one, but meets all the others. If that imaginary person seems desirable, revise your list accordingly.

- Ask for what you want, but be realistic. Ninety-five percent of singles chase after the same five percent: the beautiful, rich, and accomplished. Don't expect to get 100 percent of what you want. Expect rather to discover someone who turns out to be just right for you.

Prioritize your essential qualities, the *E* items:

1. appreciates me
2. nonsmoker
3. sensitive
4. kind
5. honest
6. physically fit
7. warm/caring/affectionate
8. intelligent

Note: If you ask your friends who are happily married if their spouses fit the image they had for their ideal mate, you'll find that most initially didn't. People who are inflexible tend to remain single.

Chapter 5

Creating a Successful Ad

Online personal ads tend to be much longer than their newspaper counterparts. So you can include a lot of information about yourself and what you're looking for. This chapter should help you to decide what to include in your ad. I address questions such as:

- What should you say about yourself?

- What should you leave out?

- What phrases turn people on and off?

- When are white lies acceptable?

- How can you get people to notice your ad?

- What should you write in your headline?

What to Put in Your Ad

I wish I could give you one tip that you could follow to find your lifelong mate online. Unfortunately, there is no one simple path.

Look at other ads, especially those of your competitors—people of your sex seeking the same sort of people who interest you. Gather up the ones that you like. What appeals to you about those ads?

Exercise: Which Ads Appeal To You

A career counselor once told me to look through a newspaper and to find the job ads that interested me, regardless of whether I was qualified for them. She advised me to learn what I want in a job by analyzing the types of positions that appealed to me. Why not do the same with online ads?

Look at some ads and answer the following questions:

- What are your first impressions of the people who wrote these profiles?

- What phrases grab your attention?

- What phrases turn you off?

- Which ads make you want to ask or tell the author something?

- How do you think the ads can be improved?

- What about the ad most appeals to you?

Sell Yourself

When you place an ad, you are marketing yourself. Describe your endearing qualities, the ones that make you special. Share what's wonderful about you and your life. Tell why another person would want to be with you.

Emphasize your strengths and what you have to offer. Don't dwell on your limitations. Show people why it's to their advantage to get to know you. That's what Anna did:

I've sailed the Atlantic, modeled for the
L.L. Bean catalog, qualified as a Cordon
Bleu chef, read the classics, tasted the
best wines in Europe, and owned my own
businesses. But I'm still searching for
the true love of my life. One of my degrees
is in Marine Biology (when I was four I
wanted to be a sea otter when I grew up).
I love water and the outdoors but also
love getting dressed up in a little black
dress and "doing" the city. I ADORE being
feminine. I'm tall, leggy, athletic, with
reddish-blond hair, hazel eyes, a friendly
smile, and freckles on my nose. I'm in
great shape--(mountain biking may have
something to do with that--I intend never
to look close to my age). Some of my other
passions include a great circle of friends
and family all over the world, reading
(The Economist is my favorite magazine...but
I never miss a chance to peek at People
in the checkout line), animals (Labradors
are my weakness--I have a black female
puppy), Paris, fresh flowers, copper pans,
islands, mountains, horses, Van Morrison,
Celtic and Blues music, single malts, hiking
(I live in a cabin on 100 acres on top
of a mountain in wine country) ... but
most of all I love laughing, having fun,
and trying to see the Monty Python/Gary
Larson side of life while experiencing
the sensuous hedonistic pleasures that
life has to offer. I'm described by my
companions as an outgoing, romantic, optimist

> ... never boring and a true friend. So,
> what am I looking for? You are tall, handsome
> (yes--I admit to being slightly superficial),
> sexy, savvy, successful and make me laugh.
> In an ideal world you drive a Land Rover
> or Jeep, wear Eddie Bauer/Gap/Banana Republic
> type duds and Ray Bans. (I'm not--and
> probably never will be--into beards, New
> Age/Left/Vegetarian types.) You are well
> educated (streetwise and academically),
> and someone who not only knows how to dream
> but has experience in turning dreams into
> reality. Are you for me?

Anna, who is forty-eight, is delighted with the responses that she received. Several men offered to fly out to San Francisco to meet her. After she talked on the telephone for about thirty hours with George, he flew down from British Columbia. They are now talking about getting married. If it hadn't been for putting their ads online, their paths never would have crossed.

Be Honest

Honesty should be a guiding principle for personal ads. You may get more responses if you subtract thirty pounds from your weight or add three inches to your height, but what happens the first time you meet? Your date's thought will be: "You lied."

As a research project, I decided to see whether I would receive more responses if I lied by reporting my age as lower than it is. My first dilemma was what age to list. I was 41. I considered listing my age as 34, 35, 36, or 37. I chose 35 because I thought men who were interested in having children would prefer women who are at most 35.

My next dilemma was deciding when to reveal my true age to the wonderful men who contacted me. The initial few people who responded I told in my first e-mail. A few of these men never wrote back. Consequently, I decided to tell men when I first met them so they would see for themselves that I could easily pass for less than my age.

When I met David, he innocently asked when I had studied at UC Berkeley, thinking that we must have been there at the same time—but I had been there six years earlier. Rather than tell another lie, I told him my age. Luckily, David was understanding. Many men would have been turned off.

Lying about my age, I received nearly fifty percent more responses than when I reported my age accurately. But regardless of when I confessed the truth, I felt bad about lying. The men I met might think, "Since she lied about her age, what else might she be concealing?" Instead of lying, it would be better to say that I prefer men my own age or younger. Now I understand why people advise being honest. Lies tend to get you into trouble. Be honest. That's exactly what Florence did:

```
Look, if you want a shallow Cindy Crawford
clone, that's not me.  I'm more a case
of still waters running deep.  What do
I mean by that?  I'm a large, quiet woman
on the surface, with a strong passionate
undercurrent.  Well, to tell you a little
more about me:  I sometimes refer to myself
as an original WYSIWYG[1] woman.  I have brown
hair with a few silver threads, which I
have no intention of coloring.  My eyes
are hazel (standard brown/green/blue-grey)
and my skin is fair.  I'm 5'10", and currently
about 240, although that is falling.  I
prefer old VWs to new BMWs, and don't do
```

---

[1]WYSIWYG is short for *What You See is What You Get*. But I would have advised Florence to spell this out; not everyone will understand if you use abbreviations.

sushi. I would rather cuddle than do aerobics,
go someplace like Yosemite than Las Vegas,
take a quiet walk with someone special
to roller-blading (never been, probably
never will), and have an intimate dinner
for two than a formal banquet for two hundred.
I'm intelligent and strong-willed, but
also the most supportive person you'll
probably ever meet. I am a stickler for
integrity. I try my darnedest not to deceive
others, won't tolerate being deceived,
and refuse to be a party to an innocent
person (like a wife) being deceived. I
am looking for someone confident enough
in himself to take me on, and accept and
appreciate me for who I am. If you're
interested and not allergic to cats, drop
me a line!

This ad served its purpose. It attracted many men, including
Mark, Florence's husband.

When you describe yourself honestly and accurately, you tend
to receive fewer responses because you don't compare favorably
with most other people who exaggerate their good points. Should
you stop being honest? No. Your goal should be the *quality* of
responses, not their *quantity*. You may need to emphasize more
of your good qualities, or change words that may be turning
people off, but you'll do best in the long run if you are honest.

Grab Their Attention

As they do in a newspaper, a bold headline for an ad grabs people's attention. When Andy, after his divorce, wrote his first ad,
he used the headline "First Date in Ten Years!?" The headline
was true and captured the mixed feelings that Andy had about

being single again. He got over a dozen responses!

Here are examples of catchy headlines:

- I WANT IT ALL!!! (And here's what you get in return)
- Humor, Brains, and Heart—for Long-Term Partnership and Family
- Just Your Basic Nice Guy (it could be worse!)
- Looking for Knight for All My Nights to Come
- Olympic Medalist, Harvard MBA, Ph.D., Model, Brain Surgeon, and Fortune 100 CEO Seeking Goddess
- My Computer's Connected, but I'm Not
- Looking for Collaborator: Will it be a romance, nonfiction, or comedy?
- Looking for a woman who is willing to lie about how we met

Show Your Personality and Your Passions

Shine! You'll be more likely to attract the sort of person you want. Use words, phrases, and language that represent you well.

Instead of listing your outstanding qualities, demonstrate them. If you like poetry, include an example. Tell a story about yourself and the person whom you hope to meet:

```
In my dream, we're walking on a long beach
in the moonlight.  I'm singing you a song
as you run about looking for pieces of
ocean glass.  You have a few more than
my own 28 years, but your healthful energy
makes you seem younger.  You have sand
in your hair and I remark on it mischievously.
You laugh and kick sand at me.  I chase
you and catch you because you want me to.
```

> I touch your cheek, you kiss my hand. And
> then I wake up. Where are you?

This ad says little about the author other than his age; instead, it paints an appealing picture with romantic and playful images.

Make your ad stand out so that it will be noticed. Lots of people say they love taking long walks on the beach, they're well educated, they've successful, they look younger than they are, and they're in great shape. Saying only that in a personal ad isn't likely to inspire someone to contact you, and it certainly won't make you stand out from the crowd.

Add color, imagination, and pizzazz. Show your passions. Describe the feeling you get when you ski down a mountain or meditate. Instead of just listing your desirable traits, such as intelligence or a sense of humor, use them. In this ad, Elaine describes herself as a car:

> *Headline:* Little Red Triumph Spitfire in
> Need of Maintenance!
>
> Are you good with your hands? I hope so,
> because I'm a little Spitfire who needs
> a good mechanic. I'm a little slow starting
> in the morning, but once I get my motor
> running .... All right, I have a couple
> of rust spots, but I'm still maneuverable
> and a lot of fun. Applications for mechanic
> and driver eagerly awaited!
>
> *Profile:*
>   *Ethnicity:* Caucasian
>   *Body Type:* Average (trim, nice headlights)
>   *Height:* 5 ft., 2 in.

Elaine was bombarded with responses after placing this ad. One guy volunteered "to put her up on a rack and check her out."

Mark described himself and what he's looking for:

```
I'm an entrepreneur at heart but am currently
employed. (I've made my first million,
but not for me.) I like exploring mysterious
small bookstores, viewing double features
in intimate cinemas, experiencing music
from every corner of the earth, taking
culinary adventures with good friends (I
cook!), going to museums, street fairs,
and more. I am interested in history,
science, science fiction, the future, and
the mind. I preferred "Goedel, Escher,
Bach" to "A Brief History of Time." I have
a house, a cat, and a beard (I use conditioner
on it to keep it silky [the beard, not
the cat]). I'm looking for friends. I
hope to find an equal partner, a friend
and lover, with whom to create a family
of our own. Most of all, I want to enjoy
life with a special someone. A walking
tour of the city is great, but walking,
holding hands, is even better. By the
fireplace on a foggy night is OK, but cuddling
with someone I care about is even better.
I seek loyalty, fidelity, and a happy someone
to cuddle in the evening and in the morning.
```

Florence thought the ad had "wonderful quirky bits of humor." She particularly liked Mark's comment about his use of conditioner. Now Florence and Mark are husband and wife.

Be Specific

Include hard data (facts such as your age, height, body type, educational background, profession), and your interests, say why

someone would want to be with you, and what you're looking for.
Make your ad stand out. Be expressive. Name recent movies and
books you like. Mention your favorite music styles or musicians.
If you enjoy going out to Thai restaurants or bicycling, say so.
Your message not only conveys information about you, but also
provides topics for people to talk about when they respond.
I remember the first personal ad I placed. It was in the *Jewish
Bulletin*, a weekly San Francisco newspaper. I knew my mother
read the ads in the *Jewish Bulletin*, because she looked for men
for me. I didn't want her to know that I had placed an ad. So I
included few details that would indicate that I wrote it.

```
Good looking and in great shape. Enjoy movies,
socializing with friends, going out. Seeking
a man who enjoys the same.
```

People who read this ad didn't know much about me. Few
responded and those who did didn't interest me. The moral of
this story: *If you want to meet people who would be interested in
you, include specific information about yourself.* That's exactly
what Fred did. Here's what he wrote:

```
[Stardate 970523.9: Saturday. I wake up to
National Public Radio replacing the light jazz
I heard falling asleep. Crawling over Heavy
Metal on way to bathroom, my eyes meet my bearded
face in the mirror. Time for Peet's coffee and
a bagel. Mind roams to last week's sushi feast
and Shawn Colvin concert--very fun time. Hmmm.
Lyrics mingle as I begin marinating the food
for the barbie, this time zinfindel, garlic,
rosemary, and basil. Dog looks at me "rollerblade
today?" as I gaze out on the patio--I should
put a hot tub there. Wonder if I should rent
the newest anime video tonight, or maybe Fargo.
```

```
Ugh, work tomorrow on design and patents for
next-generation cable modems. *sigh* startups....
Maybe I'll give up this vice president job.  Good
thing KFOG acoustic music tomorrow morning.]
I'm seeking open-minded woman for sharing witty
friendship and companionship, balanced conversation,
active communication, fun times (maybe a few
wild times...), mutual appreciation and respect
for each other's personal growth and interests.
Comfortable with and without makeup.  More about
me:  compassionate, honest, good listener, creative,
Monty Python, classic movies (Grant & Hepburn,
Hitchcock), low fat, good and bad humor movies,
SciFi, TV animation (Duckman, The Tick, SouthPark,
The Simpsons), Arnold, art, theater, affectionate,
deep oakey Chardonney otherwise "life is too
short to drink white wine," single malt (with
good cigar on rare occasions), computers, 3D
games, past skydiver, pilot, reading, Internet,
scuba, biking, skiing, dogs, clothing optional
beaches, travel for work, healthy, good teeth,
brown hair, 4runner, toys, massage, Pippin, Phantom,
comedy, Gallagher, meditation, tools, not political,
"42", anything twice.
```

Tell What You Want

In your ad, list those characteristics that are essential to you,
those from the list you made on page 37. This is particularly
important for women because there are men who will answer
practically any ad posted by a woman. If you get more responses
to your ad than you can handle, consider also listing the characteristics that you consider desirable. Do you want to spend time
sifting through responses that are of no interest to you? Here are
a few examples taken from ads that state what they want:

- I'm seeking someone who goes for what
he wants and who isn't intimidated by an
outgoing, confident, intelligent woman
who says what's on her mind.

- Looking for a serious long-term committed
relationship, preferably involving tying
the knot.

- Extra points for someone who loves cooking.

- Please don't respond if you're on Prozac
and in therapy.

- I won't tolerate body piercings, tattoos,
B&D, S&M, spectator sports, or restricted
diets. It would be icing on the cake if
you were Jewish, but not fanatic about
it. You could meet me for weekday lunches
near Alameda.

- I'd like to meet a woman with intellectual
curiosity, which isn't to be confused with
(but isn't incompatible with) an accumulation
of degrees (my bedroom resembles an early
version of the mythical warehouse for Amazon.com).
A love of the outdoors is also important.
I've met people whose idea of outdoor activity
is reading the New York Times Book Review
in an outdoor cafe--good clean fun, I agree,
but what I had in mind was more like hiking
in Nepal or the Alps (Yosemite would suffice).

Prioritize Items

My friend Brian's ad states that he likes hiking, bicycling, sailing, skiing, wind surfing, backpacking, horseback riding, ball-

room dancing, rock climbing, swimming, basketball, volleyball, racquetball, and tennis. How does he have time for all these activities? And does he do anything other than sports? Don't make a laundry list of every thing you've ever done! Choose a few of your favorites, and communicate your passion about them.

Words to Use and Words to Avoid

Choose your words with care. The following phrases turn off most women:

> well hung
> great in bed
> I'd love to satisfy you
> sexually insatiable

Women tend to prefer phrases such as:

affectionate	great hugger	communicative
loves cuddling	romantic	sensitive
giving	caring	loves cooking
thoughtful	monogamous	
interested in commitment		

Women tend to get more responses when they say they have great figures and when they allude to sex by including words such as

> sensual   sexy   passionate

Tom noticed that women who mention *tantra yoga*[2] in their profile, usually take it out after a couple of days. Tom suspects that those women get completely bombarded with responses.

Weight is a touchy area. A woman who thinks she needs to lose at least five pounds, and that includes most women, may be intimidated by criteria such as:

---

[2]Tantra yoga is a type of yoga with a sexual orientation.

    thin   trim   fit   athletic

Instead, I suggest that men describe their preferences with words
like

    large but not fat
    average
    height and weight proportional
    anything from thin to could-lose-a-few-pounds

When you promote yourself, be careful not to go overboard.
It's better to use "intelligent" or "well educated" than to say
"brilliant" and thus to appear vain. It's best to write a clever,
literate ad that lets readers can figure out that you're intelligent. Saying you're smart can make you appear otherwise. Self-
deprecating humor can be charming, but don't go overboard
there either.

Use caution before revealing say, an ugly divorce, large debt,
or substance abuse. Such personal matters are best discussed
after you've gotten to know each other. Mentioning these matters
too early can signal a lack of tact.

You may also have pet peeves that are hard to talk about
in an ad. Perhaps you've had a bad experience with someone
who has strong religious beliefs, or with a recovering alcoholic.
An ad that says "no fundamentalists or members of AA" might
be an accurate reflection of your desires, but be aware that such
words may make you appear rigid and narrow-minded even to
people who aren't fundamentalists or AA members. *Avoid being
negative in your ad.*

Finally, don't place an ad when you hate yourself or you're
mad at the opposite sex. Your anger will show through in your
ad and in your e-mail.

Sometimes Less is More

Some services offer ads that are up to 500 or 2000 characters long;
other services allow you to place an ad of any length. You don't

have to resort to the curt and cryptic abbreviations typically used in newspaper personals. Although there may be no restriction on the length, there's no need to disclose everything about yourself. A long list of requirements can make you seem overly picky and might scare away someone you'd like.

Use your ad to entice, just as companies do. Note that in their ads for a laser printer, Hewlett-Packard doesn't list the complete hardware specifications. Instead, they give you hints about what the device can do, show you samples of what it can produce, and get customers to share reasons why they are satisfied.

Share your best points: say, what you like about yourself and what your friends like about you. Say enough that people get a feeling for your personality and wit, and learn a few of your interests. Someone who wants to find out more can write to you.

What About Your Shortcomings?

In selling yourself, feel free to list your quirks and dislikes, if you feel they are an important part of you. But, as in a job interview, use caution when saying negative things about yourself. If you reveal your negative points, you probably will receive fewer responses, but those that you get will be interested in you for the way you are.

Dean Esmay began using the Usenet[3] personals in 1995, where he eventually met the woman he married. Along the way, he learned from his many experiences. To share them, he wrote *The Straight FAQ: One Straight Male's Thoughts and Advice on Successful Use of Internet Personals.*[4] It's a lighthearted, "one guy to another" article, mixing humor with blunt, straight-to-the-point advice that emphasizes the importance of being honest

---

[3]Usenet is a distributed bulletin board system. You can read about it on page 178.

[4]The complete article can be found at http://www.syndicomm.com/straight-faq.html on the Web.

and being yourself. Here are his recommendations of what to include in your ad:

> If you *are* obese, male or female, *just say so in your ad*. Don't be afraid of this. You're preparing yourself *and* whomever you meet for a letdown if you're not blunt on this subject. If you're fat, just say, "Hey, I'm queen sized" or "I'm John Goodman sized" or "I'm a Rubenesque woman" or something like that. Or just say "I'm fat." The point is, *be honest!*
>
> We live in a culture that values thinness, but there are a lot, and I mean *a whole lot*, of people out there who genuinely *don't* care about weight. There are even a good number of people out there who *like* fatness and find it attractive.
>
> Don't be timid about it. If you're overweight, be forthright and don't weasel around the subject, unless you look forward to the prospect of being embarrassed, disappointed, and hurt. Lots and lots of people will love you if you're fat, and you're not giving them a chance if you don't *tell* them you're fat right up front.
>
> Don't say anything that a face to face encounter will make you out to be a liar.

Consider starting your ad by describing your positives so as to mitigate any perceived negatives. In the following ad, Andy conveys that he is in decent shape and has a sense of humor, but doesn't cook and is into computers:

```
Although I'm in decent shape, it's more
from a high metabolism than regular exercise
or a healthy diet.  (One of my bachelor
jokes:  "All my standard recipes start
the same way:  'Pull tab, lift corner to
```

```
vent.'" [Yeah, I wrote that.])  I did do
the gym thing while in art school though.
Sometimes my honest and geeky nature shows
itself in clumsy, nonromantic ways.
```

My friend Sally, who is forty-two years old, didn't think that many men would be interested in her. I suspected some men using online matchmaking services just might want to meet someone in her position, so I wrote this ad for her:

```
Handle:  SomethingExtra
Headline:  Want a child?

I want to be up front about this, so that
you won't be surprised when you first see
me.  I'm pregnant.  I've always wanted
a child so I took the necessary steps to
have one.  Besides children, I enjoy west
coast swing and cooking.  I work in the
health care industry.  If you want to know
more, please write.
```

Sally and I were pleasantly surprised that a dozen men responded, some who were interested in Sally and others who just wanted to share their experiences of being a single parent.

Let people know up front who you are. If you're out of shape, you're pregnant, or you smoke, say so. You are more apt to find someone who doesn't mind—or appreciates—those characteristics. Also it's better to find out sooner than later whether such things bother someone. Sometimes, it's better to lower people's expectations, so that they will be pleasantly surprised when they meet you.

Include a Photograph

If you want more people to look at your ad, include a picture. Don't include just any picture. Pick one in which you're smiling, happy, and relaxed. More people look at ads that have photographs. Even people who are not good-looking do better when they include a picture. It changes "I have no idea what to expect" to "I can live with that." Photographs reduce uncertainty.

Although you may have looked better five or ten years ago, use a recent photograph. If you use an old photograph or touch up a new one, you may disappoint people when they meet you.

Here are several reasons for not including a photograph:

- You don't want people you know to realize that you're using an online matchmaking service.

- You are already receiving more than enough responses.

- You want to be judged on your personality rather than your looks. Both attractive and average looking people feel this way.

- You don't want strangers to recognize you.

- You think you're homely.

Mark has a friend who considers herself unattractive. She finds it painful being rejected when people meet her face to face. So she includes her photograph so that men who are put off by her looks can reject her without her knowing about it.

Nathan, who included a photograph of himself riding a horse, had a completely different experience.

> Since I'm a scientist, I experimented with the profiles trying to learn what works. To my surprise the only thing that improves my rate of response is including my photo.

Running Multiple Ads

Meeting many prospects increases your chances of finding someone who's right for you. Experiment with different approaches;
place different ads on several services to increase the chances of
your getting responses from a variety of people.

Another tactic for increasing responses is to place more than
one ad on your favorite service. Few services block you from
signing up for multiple accounts. They are interested in getting
as many people as possible on their service, especially if you're
paying for each account. However, services that allow you to
send e-mail from your own computer account or through your
Internet Service Provider require you to have a distinct e-mail
address for each of your accounts. Consider if I listed my address as `capulet@dnai.com` for an account with handle `Active`
and for a second account with handle `BigBrownEyes`. If I were
to send an e-mail message from `capulet@dnai.com`, the service
would not know whether I intended that it be from `Active` or
`BigBrownEyes`. Consequently, online matchmaking services that
allow you to send e-mail from your own computer require that
you provide them with an e-mail address that is distinct from
all others on their system. America Online (AOL) allows you to
create different user names for your account. If you only have
one computer account and you want to sign up for more than
one account on a matchmaking service, then consider signing up
with a free e-mail service such as Hotmail, Rocketmail, or Juno,
which I describe on page 91.

Experiment. Show different parts of your personality or emphasize your various interests. I signed up for a matchmaking
service and placed an ad. Immediately, I received about a dozen
responses. After it was posted on the service for a couple of
months, my ad grew stale; the few responses that I did receive
were from men who didn't sound interesting. Rather than con-
tinuing to wait around for men to write to me, I decided to send
e-mail to several men. I looked for men who seemed gregari-

ous, active, intelligent, kind, and witty, and who lived within an hour's drive. I selected five and sent them e-mail letting them know that what they wrote caught my eye.

I needed something to distract me from checking for replies every half hour. Writing a new profile for myself would do the job. If I kept the same handle but changed my description, men who remembered my original handle would not bother to check it out, since they had seen what I had written before. So I decided to create a brand new entry with a different handle. I wanted to be treated like a new woman on the service. I wanted to show a different side of my personality—a part more lighthearted and fun.

What should I say? To get ideas, I checked out other profiles. At first I looked at profiles of women who lived in the San Francisco Bay Area. I came across one ad that mentioned the computer-oriented comic strip character Dilbert, and Fry's, a store that sells computers and electronic hardware. I suspected that the author received many responses, because many of my male friends enjoy shopping at Fry's and find Dilbert amusing.

I scanned profiles of women in other parts of the country. I started my search in New York City. Why New York? I like cities. I hoped to find other women who like living in a city. New York City is sure to have high-powered, witty, and competitive women, who are assertive, outspoken, independent—and perhaps work in advertising and write alluring ads. In my search, I came across an ad that caught my eye.

Headline: SMART, SEXY, SWEET, AND RELATIVELY SANE

Are you saying to yourself, "What the heck (ooh, haven't said 'heck' since... well, since ever) am I doing reading the personals?" So am I. I can't for the life of me figure out why my Knight In Shining Armor hasn't

ridden in on his horse and carried me off
into the sunset. All I can think is that
maybe Fate's been saving me for a guy who
prefers some other form of transportation.
Like maybe the subway?

Although this ad didn't say much about the woman's interests, it showed that she is self-confident, down to earth, and romantic, and has a sense of humor. I thought her ad was great.

After considering several ads, I decided to use the knight-in-shining armor ad as a basis for my ad. It had personality and the author had fun with the text. It was the best one that I ran across. I revised the ad to fit me.

Headline: SMART, SEXY, SWEET, AND RELATIVELY SANE

Are you saying to yourself, "What am I
doing reading the personals?" So am I.
I can't for the life of me figure out why
my knight in shining armor hasn't yet ridden
in on his horse and carried me off into
the sunset. Perhaps fate's been saving
me for a guy who prefers some other form
of transportation and more comfortable
attire, and who would rather live in a
city than in a castle or a place in the
country. I know this sounds terribly immodest
of me (and this whole anonymous thing is
making me frightfully bold), but I'm a
technical professional who's smart and
well-educated (I have degrees from Berkeley
and Stanford), cute, healthy, and sexy
(beyond being disease free, I practice
a healthy lifestyle: No smoking, no illegal
drugs, little red meat, and regular exercise).

> I'm also passionate, well-traveled, published,
> independent, single, and relatively sane.
> So what's the problem? My mother thinks
> I'm too picky. Well, I don't want to settle
> for anything but a mind-blowing, intense,
> monogamous, intimate relationship. If
> you're someone who likes himself, isn't
> married, doesn't have a thing for his ex,
> and doesn't have a balance on his credit
> cards, drop me a line. I may just be your
> damsel who's done with distress.

Wanting a handle that showed I was a bit out of the ordinary, I selected **Fervent**. According to the Webster Digital dictionary, it means "very hot: glowing" or "exhibiting or marked by great intensity of feeling." Both those definitions sounded good to me.

Although I'm five feet, four and a half inches, I listed my height as five feet, four inches so those who had seen my original ad, where I listed myself at being five feet, five inches, wouldn't suspect that I had written both.

The response was amazing. Within hours I had received a half dozen responses; within a few days I had received over fifty; within a fortnight, I had received 100. At least a dozen of the replies were from men whose profiles I found appealing.

I was pleasantly surprised that two of the five men to whom I had written earlier that morning responded to my new profile! Both men appeared more interested in **Fervent**'s profile than in my original one, whose handle was **Izzi**. What was I going to do? Should I have **Fervent** and **Izzi** write to them separately? If I told them that both were created by me, would that dilute their enthusiasm for **Fervent**? How would I feel if I were writing to two men and then found out that they were the same person? To avoid an awkward situation, I wrote those two men and informed them that I had two profiles. They both seemed pleased with my honesty and interested in meeting me in person, but one of them asked why Izzi was an inch taller. I explained that Fervent preferred wearing shoes with low heels.

How to Write Your Ad

In preparation for writing your ad, review your answers to the exercise on what you desire (page 36) and to the exercise concerning what you offer (page 33).

Exercise: Draft an Ad

Write a paragraph in which you show that you're creative, clever, thoughtful, or whatever you are. Describe the person whom you are seeking, as well as what you don't want. Get a draft written on your computer. Don't worry about it not being quite right.

If you're having difficulty figuring out what to say, you're in good company. Most people feel uncomfortable with self-promotion. But remember, people who write ads are people who don't want to stay single and who are willing to do something to change their situation. Are you such a person?

Proofread, Proofread, Proofread!

Re-evaluate. Could your ad be putting off people by stating too many requirements? Do you come across as too nondescript? Are you describing yourself accurately? Does your ad make you sound desperate, overly serious, superficial, undesirable, or unappealing?

Do you want to appear sloppy or poorly educated? If not, before placing your ad online, check for spelling, grammar, and punctuation errors. Read it out loud.

Now put it online. Browse it to see what it will look like to other members. If it doesn't look right, fix it.

See what response you get. Tweak your ad every now and then. Experiment to see what works and what doesn't. Are you

attracting people who interest you? If so, great! It's working.
What if you haven't received any bites? It could be that you're
too impatient. It takes some people a few days or even a couple
of weeks to respond. Most men receive zero to a half dozen
responses to their ads. Consider yourself lucky if you're a man
and you receive over a dozen quality responses.

No Good Responses?

What if you've posted your ad for weeks and haven't received
any good responses? Here are several things you can do:

- *Get feedback.* — Show your ad to friends, both men and
  women. Ask for feedback on how you can improve it.

  - Don't rush to accept every criticism or piece of advice.
    Listen to criticism, but also listen to your heart. Even
    if you don't accept the advice that someone gives you,
    just hearing another perspective may give you new
    ideas for improving your ad.

  - You may worry that the people you ask for advice
    will think you're weird for placing personal ads. But
    online services provide a perfectly valid way of meet-
    ing people. Consult friends who are open-minded and
    genuinely want to help you. Also, try asking people
    whom you meet online.

- *Try another service.* — Perhaps the service on which you've
  placed the ad doesn't get much traffic.

- *Be patient.* — As Dean Esmay says:

    Remember the audience isn't static. There's a
    constant influx of new [people], and there's a con-
    stant outflow, too. So remember, you may not

find anyone at first, but if you're patient and you keep at it, chances are good you'll eventually get nibbles.

- *Reach farther.* — The reason you're not getting any responses may have nothing to do with the contents of your ad. Although you can write to anyone in the world with an Internet connection, many people prefer to write to people who live nearby, so that they won't have to travel far to get together. If you live far from any major metropolitan areas, your responses may be limited. If you don't mind traveling, let people know in your ad that you're willing to travel to meet them.

- *Be responsive.* — Are you willing to answer all responses you receive? If so, consider mentioning that in your ad.

- *Initiate contact.* — Write to people you find interesting. For suggestions on how to respond to an ad, read Chapter 8.

Too Many Responses?

You may get more responses than you can handle. In that case, it's likely that many of the responses are from people who don't interest you. Rewrite your ad, shifting emphasis, making it more specific. If you're getting responses from people who are too young or too old, stress your desired age range. Try adding entries from your desirable-list characteristics. Including more of your unusual quirks or interests can also reduce the chaff without losing the wheat.

However, if you are a woman, some men may write to you regardless of what you put in your profile. Just discard responses that seem inappropriate, telling the sender that you don't seem like a good match.

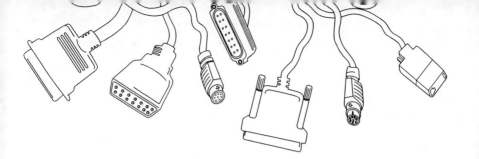

Part II

Making Connections

Myth: When you look for love, you'll never find it.

The harder you look, the luckier you get.

There are people online right now looking for someone like you. Online dating creates opportunities for connections that otherwise would not happen. Check it out.

Chapter 6

Finding Hearts Online

In cyberspace, just as in the physical world, there are heart-throbs, jerks, sweeties, gems, nerds, intellectuals, slackers, hunks, and crazies. In this chapter, I tell you how to find the great ones and how to avoid the losers.

Online dating opens up a wealth of possibilities. There are millions of people from whom to choose. You can connect with people of different ages, ethnicities, and religions who live in your neighborhood, in another part of the country, or on a different continent. But reading though the ads can be time consuming. A computer can scan text files millions of times faster than you can. So let the computer sift through all the ads and inform you which ones meet your criteria. Then, you can review those ads and select the ones that you wish to pursue.

Setting Your Criteria

On many matchmaking services, you answer questions about yourself and specify criteria that you're seeking in a mate. Then, you can instruct the computer to find your matches—those people who meet your criteria. As you can see in the following stories, changing your criteria can have a significant effect on your number of matches. When you use two-way matching (finding people who meet your criteria and you theirs), changing how you classify yourself also affects your matches.

No Matches

To meet more people (as I mentioned on page 57), I ran two ads simultaneously. After placing my ad for `Fervent`, I decided to look at my matches: men whose criteria I met and who met my criteria, which were that they lived within forty miles of my home and were atheist or Jewish, not overweight, nonsmokers, light drinkers, and open to having children. I pushed the button on my screen labeled *Match Now*. To my astonishment, no profiles matched. Forty-six men matched my original profile, whose matching criteria were similar, if not identical. What was going on?

I decided to experiment and to give slightly different input to see whether the output changed. I broadened my search criteria to include Christians. I selected the *Match Now* button and the system informed me that three profiles matched mine—again, fewer than I expected. I read the long description of the first entry:

```
I love live-theater, good restaurants,
and cooking.  I fight off the middle age
spread by bicycling several times a week.
Due to old-fashioned midwest values, I'm
HIV-.  Would love to meet someone of similar
interests; someone who is active, dependable,
attractive, fit, healthy self-image, straight
acting and appearing, and enjoys life.
```

The letters HIV jumped out at me. This ad was the first that I had come across that listed HIV status. Then I reread the ad, and noticed the phrase "straight acting and appearing." What did that mean? Just then it occurred to me that I was looking at an ad of a man who was interested in meeting men. In my haste at learning about this guy, I had skipped over his short description:

```
37 year-old male, located in SF Bay Area,
seeking 25 to 45 year-old male for activity
partner, short-term relationship, or long-term
relationship.
```

How dumb of me. I had forgotten to check the box to indicate that I was female. Since more men sign up, the site designed their software to default to male. So the system assumed I was male, since I hadn't indicated that I was female.

I learned from this experience: (1) be sure to check the gender box (after I did, forty-six men matched), (2) many more men are looking for women than for men, and (3) there are online more gay Christians than gay Jews and atheists interested in having children!

Debugging Your Love Life

At one of my talks, a thirtysomething, six feet, one inch tall man named Keith, who lives in Silicon Valley, mentioned that only one or two women match his criteria. I wondered what Keith specified to get so few matches. Plenty of women in the San Francisco Bay Area are on the same online matchmaking service as Keith. After my talk, we went to a computer so that I could take a look at his profile. When I reviewed it, I couldn't immediately tell why the system returned few women when he asked for his two-way matches. Here are his description of himself and his criteria for a desired match:

Description of himself:

Age:	33
Ethnicity:	Caucasian
Religion:	Other than those listed (not practicing)
Body Type:	Slim/slender
Height:	6 ft., 1 in. (185 cm)
Smoking:	Don't smoke
Drinking:	Drink socially/occasionally
Children:	Don't have children
Plans for Children:	Don't want children

His criteria for a desired match are:

Maximum Distance:	40 miles (64 km) from you
Age:	28 to 36 year-old
Gender & Relationship:	Female for activity partner, short-term relationship, or long-term relationship
Ethnicity:	Caucasian
Body Type:	Athletic; average; or slim/slender
Smoking:	Doesn't smoke
Drinking:	Doesn't drink or drinks socially/occasionally
Children:	Doesn't have children
Plans for Children:	Doesn't want children

I again decided to experiment; I changed one of the inputs to see how it affected his number of matches. With his original criteria, the system reported that he had two matches. I thought that women in their late thirties might be less interested in having children. So I extended his upper desired age range from thirty-six to forty. Two more women matched. Figuring that women might prefer someone with meat on his bones to a skinny man, we changed his description of his body type from "slim/slender" to "average," but that caused no substantial change in the matches. Figuring that women who are undecided about having children may be open to not having children, Keith broadened his search to include those who specified their plans for children as "undecided." His number of matches increased significantly. The system now reported forty-two matches. What does this story tell us?

1. How you state your criteria can have a substantial effect on your matches.

2. Few women in their thirties who live in the San Francisco Bay Area state that they don't want children, but there are a fair number of women who state that they are undecided about having children.

3. You'll probably match more people if you state your plans for children as "undecided" instead of "doesn't want children."

Deciding What's Important

Many women, especially those who are slim and in their twenties or thirties, get bombarded with responses to their ads. Some women have complained to me that they receive over 100 responses. So that fewer men will write, many women narrow their criteria. They think about characteristics they dream of their partner having. Many women who want to be more selective typically exclude overweight, bald, or short men. Many men typically exclude overweight and older women. Are they the people you want to exclude? Are these people not worth considering? Check out their profiles. See whether you're overlooking great catches. Are tall men with full heads of hair or thin young women significantly more desirable?

There's a more useful way of narrowing your search. Specify your criteria in terms of the characteristics that you consider essential. Look at the people who match. If your search comes up with more matches than you can handle, change your criteria or your description of yourself. After each change, review profiles that match your criteria. For example, if you listed yourself as both athletic and of average build, see whether you come up with more interesting men when you classify yourself as one or the other. Determine the criteria and the description of yourself that makes the best matches.

Scoping Out the Competition

Look at your competition—people of your gender who are seeking the same set of people as you are. In addition to giving you ideas of what to say, looking at your competition should help you to figure out how you can get noticed.

Looking at your competition may increase your chances of meeting someone. Compare people who fit your criteria with people who are looking for someone like you. To estimate my odds of meeting men on a particular matchmaking service, I compare the men who meet my criteria and with women who describe themselves as being similar to me. For example, I count the number of men who meet my criteria—live within forty miles of my home, don't smoke, don't drink or drink occasionally, are Jewish or atheist, and are between thirty-five and forty-five years old. I then count the number of women who are are similar to me (approximately my age, my height, don't smoke) and I compare the two numbers. If there is a large number of men compared to women, then I use the service. If there are significantly more women, I look at other services to see whether I can find one where the ratios are more favorable.

How to Avoid Losers

There are people out there having fun pretending that they're people they aren't. Some people lie (or don't tell the complete truth) about their age, height, weight, gender, number of children, marital status, or employment. Other people include photographs that are over five years old.

Although it might be obvious in a face-to-face meeting that a man is over fifty, he can claim to be thirty-five years old just to see who he might meet. Some men who are shorter than five feet, nine inches list their height in shoes or standing on their tip toes. Some people report "average build" when they are on the verge of, if not outright, obese. Some men masquerade as women. Some people report that they are divorced just after they have started the paperwork—or even when they are married. There's an incentive to lie: It may get you more responses. So don't believe everything you read. Watch for fakes, weirdos, criminals, and liars. If someone sounds too good to be true, he probably is. In *The Straight FAQ*, which I mentioned on page 53, Dean Esmay advises:

> Don't get your heart crushed by a liar; use caution, and don't buy too much of anything until you meet the person face to face, or at least a telephone call. Watch for the warning signs of someone yanking your chain, or wrapped up in their own fantasies and not paying attention to who you are. Don't fall in love or get your heart ripped out by someone who may just be a fantasy-woman (or man). Don't be paranoid, but make sure you don't expect too much until you meet the other person face to face.

Some advertisers leave out facts that you might consider important. I've met smokers who don't mention their habit. What someone doesn't say can be as important as what she does mention. One ad said, "Doesn't smoke tobacco." So, does she smoke dope? Some parents forget to mention their children.

One woman's headline was "Busty blonde, 25, emerging from years of celibacy, just looking to have fun." After the ad appeared, the matchmaking service called her. "Would you please pick up your messages? They're clogging the system." She wasn't busty, blonde, twenty-five, or just emerging from celibacy, but she got a boyfriend out of it anyway. (I imagine him thinking: "Well, she lied about everything ... that's the kind of woman for me!")

Most services don't screen people. If you run across an ad for a female with 36D-24-34, who loves sex, be skeptical. Not that there aren't women who fit that description, but when was the last time you met a woman who introduced herself by giving her measurements?

On the other hand, just because someone doesn't say that he's stunning doesn't mean he's a loser. Beautiful people may not announce that they are attractive. So how can you tell whether a person is good looking if he doesn't mention his looks in his ad? Beautiful people have confidence. Look for confident people: They are likely to either be arrogant or gorgeous or both.

What if an ad describes the author's negative points? It could be that he doesn't know how to sell himself. On the other hand, it could be that he is mentioning these points on purpose so his ad stands out or he could be just plain honest.

Interpreting What You Read

Here are interpretations of various words that you might run across in ads:

Meyers-Briggs Personality Typing

Some people list their Meyers-Briggs personality type

in their ad. There are sixteen different classification designated using four letters—for example, ENFJ or ISTP. People are rated on four different scales:

1. Energizing — How a person is energized. Extroversion (E) for people who draw energy from the outside world; introversion (I) for people who draw energy from their internal worlds.

2. Attending — To what a person pays attention. Sensing (S) for people who prefer taking in information through the five senses and noticing what is actual; intuition (N) for people who prefer to use their intuition.

3. Deciding — How a person decides. Thinking (T) for people who organize and structure information in a logical, objective way; feeling (F) for people who organize and structure information in a personal, value-oriented way.

4. Living — What lifestyle a person adopts. Judgment (J) for people living a planned and organized life; perception (P) for people living a spontaneous and flexible life.

♡♡♡

advanced degree — Could be an AA degree from a junior college or a doctoral from a major university.

average build — Anything from height and weight proportional to several pounds overweight.

ENFJ/P, ENTJ/P, ESFJ/P, ESTJ/P — Meyers-Briggs personality typing, described on the facing page.

financially secure — Has a job.

fortysomething — Late forties.

INFJ/P, INTJ/P, ISFJ/P, ISTJ/P — Meyers-Briggs personality typing, described on page 74.

intellectual — Prefers reading the newspaper or books to watching TV.

limited domestic skills — Doesn't have an interest in cleaning or cooking.

mature — Over fifty years old.

mensch — (from Yiddish.) A person of integrity and honor.

reliable — Probably will be on time.

self-educated — Well read but may not have a college, graduate, or even a high-school degree.

sexy — Asking for attention.

social drinker — Drinks alcoholic beverages only during social occasions; not a heavy drinker.

spiritual — Of or relating to matters of the soul of a person; has a sense that there is a higher power.

thirtysomething — Late thirties.

Terms Found in Women's Ads

assertive — Goes for what she wants.

beautiful — Don't put any credence until you meet in person.

curvaceous — Large bust and hips or perhaps slightly overweight.

dancer's body — Flat chested and/or strong legs.

full figured — Overweight.

hourglass figure — Large bust and hips and a small waist.

petite — Small size, tiny, thin, usually short.

Rubenesque — Overweight.

sensual — Enjoys physical affection (sex).

slender — Thin or skinny.

tall — At least five feet, nine inches tall.

voluptuous — Curvaceous.

zaftig — Overweight.

Terms Found in Men's Ads

bearlike — Large and hairy.

cuddly — Overweight.

gentleman — Will open a door for you (a woman) and will pay for your meal on the first few dates and not expect to have sex.

distinguished-looking — Gray hair and/or bald.

good looking — Don't put any credence until you meet in person.

handsome — Don't put any credence until you meet in person.

huggable — Large.

love handles — A few extra pounds around the waist.

medium build — Average size.

tall — At least six feet tall.

Abbreviations

Here are abbreviations that are often used in print personal ads, and that sometimes appear in online ads:

A —	Asian	**L** —	Latino or Lesbian
B —	Black	**LTR** —	Long-term relationship
Bi —	Bisexual	**M** —	Male
C —	Christian	**N/D** —	Non-drinker or no drugs
D —	Divorced	**N/S** —	Nonsmoker
F —	Female	**P** —	Professional
G —	Gay	**S** —	Single
H —	Hispanic	**W** —	White
ISO —	In search of	**WW** —	Widowed
J —	Jewish		

SWNSM — Single white nonsmoking male

S/DPF — Single or divorced professional female

Here are abbreviations used by people in the computer industry:

BTW — By the way.

f2f — Face to face (meet in person as opposed to in cyberspace).

FAQ — Frequently asked/answered questions. A compendium of lore, accumulated by an expert familiar with a topic.

FYI — For your information.

IMHO — In my humble opinion.

LJBF — Let's just be friends.

LOL — Laugh out loud. This acronym is used to indicate that you found something immensely funny.

PC — Politically correct.

RTFM — Read the f...ing manual.

YMMV — Your mileage may vary—you may get different results.

Be Flexible

Do you know your type? Do you know with what kinds of people you'd make a good match? Renée thought her type was tall, rich, Jewish, and family oriented. Perhaps it is. But there might be other men who could make her happy. Be open to meeting people who don't fit your ideal image.

Instead of looking for faults and blemishes, look for a person's good qualities. Imagine yourself as a talent scout. Try to find a potential star before he makes it big. Be flexible about what you seek.

Don't screen out people too quickly. Unless someone is unacceptable to you (a married person, an addict, a moron, a slimeball), go out with her three times before declaring that she's not for you. Most people are nervous on the first few dates. You probably won't see their true colors. Many happily married couples didn't have immediate good chemistry on their first date. So if you feel no chemistry on your first meeting, consider going on a couple of more dates. If I hadn't given David three chances, we wouldn't be together today.

Searching Capabilities

Matchmaking services provide a variety of tools for searching among their members. Here is a brief description of these capabilities.

- *Search for a specific ad* — Many services provide the capability of searching for a specific ad, so that you can find someone who has contacted you or an ad that you saw before.

- *Search by keyword* — Some services allow you to search for a particular word or phrase in an ad. Polly decided to use this feature to find men who shared her passion for hiking. She searched for ads with the word "hike." She found fourteen profiles. The search engine matched words including "hike," "hiked," and "hiker." Her search also matched a profile that said "I don't like to hike." She missed thirty-one other ads that mentioned the word "hiking." Polly should have searched on both "hike" and "hiking." *The moral of this story is that when you search for a key word, choose carefully the terms you search, and run multiple searches.*

- *Search excluding key words* — Some services allow you to search for ads that do not contain a particular word or phrase. Personally, I have no interest in astrology. So I can use this capability to exclude profiles that mention any of the twelve zodiac signs or the words "astrology" or "zodiac." But if I exclude the word "cancer," I may not see profiles of doctors or cancer survivors.

- *Search by location* — Services have implemented this feature in a variety of ways. Some services let you search for members who live within a certain distance of your home. The distance is usually computed based on zip codes, it is computed as the crow flies, instead of how you drive. Some services allow you to search by telephone area codes; other services let you specify a geographic region on a map.

Consider searching by location before you take a trip or move to a new area. That's what Tim did. He lived in Kansas City. A month before he moved to Portland, Oregon, Tim scanned the ads, wrote to several women, and lined up a date for the week that he arrived in town.

Carla, a friend of mine, contacted several people on a dating service after she interviewed for a job. She found out about the area and dating prospects. She decided not to accept the position in Billings, Montana, when she learned that there were few singles there.

- *Search by criteria* — Some services allow you to search for all members who meet a certain criterion or set of criteria (between thirty and forty years old, nonsmoker, wants children). But none that I've run across allow you to prioritize the importance of each of your criteria. For example, suppose that you would much prefer that someone live near you more than that she be within your desired age range. So you could tell the service to assign

  > 100 points for people who live within five miles,
  > 50 points for people within ten miles,
  > 20 points for people within twenty miles,
  > and so on

  and

  > 20 points for people within your desired age range,
  > 15 points for people within two years of your range,
  > 10 points for people within five years of your range,
  > and so on

  Then, the service could add up all the points for each member and show you the top point scorers first. As the number of people using online matchmaking services increases, I wouldn't be surprised if services start offering such features.

- *Searching agents* — Some services provide an agent—a program that carries out searches on your behalf. Typically you inform the agent what interests you (the criteria of your desired mate). Once activated, the agent runs searches periodically and informs you when it finds matches. Personally, I love using agents. I'd rather be notified of potential matches than periodically run searches myself.

- *Search by similarity* — A few services sort matches according to how closely someone matches you: What percentage of your responses to their multiple choice questions match

with another person. This feature is a great help if you are
looking for someone who is similar to you.

- *Search by date of last activity* — Some people sign up for a
  service and never log on again. When you get a match, it's
  best to check how recently that person has used the service.
  What's the point of spending time composing a note that
  probably won't be read by anyone except you?

Searching Using Your Own Tools

Tom grew frustrated with the tools a matchmaking service provided to its members. So Tom, who is a programmer, developed
his own tools. Few people take this tack, but I found it interesting
to learn what Tom does.

   Tom downloaded the profiles of all women in Northern California using Lynx.[1] Then, he ran a program that he wrote in a
computer language called AWK, which prints out a summary of
the profiles:

```
N smallwaist 2 23 20 24 72 72 0 0 1 2 1 1 11
M fit 0 42 42 50 63 63 1 2 1 1 0 1 10 SHARKS GOLF
N teresa 2 25 25 38 65 67 0 2 1 2 0 1 10
N whiterabbit 2 31 28 33 62 68 0 2 1 2 0 1 11
Y finally50 2 52 45 60 70 68 1 2 1 2 1 1 13
M sfc 3 49 40 60 65 67 1 2 1 1 1 1 11 SPIRIT FLUTE
M kty 0 25 27 45 62 69 1 1 1 2 0 1 9  SUSHI
N Aria 2 27 21 35 63 69 0 1 1 2 0 1 9 SHARKS
N summer3 28 23 35 65 68 0 2 1 1 0 0 9
N me_you 3 29 29 38 65 69 0 1 1 2 1 1 13
Y bottomsup 3 48 45 55 65 68 1 2 1 2 0 1 10
```

He could easily scan the summary and see which women meet his
criteria. For each profile, there are sixteen fields: match, handle,

---

[1] Lynx is a text-based browser that you can use to view text on Web sites.

distance, age, low-age-want, high-age-want, height, height-want, gates, score, keywords. The first field is either y for yes, n for no, and m for maybe. The gates, which are assigned a value of 1 if they match Tom's selection and 0 otherwise, indicate whether Tom is compatible with a woman in each of the following areas: distance, age-wanted, height-wanted, nonsmoker, body type, and desire for long-term/short-term relationship. Tom cared more about the values of some gates than he did about those of others. The final number on a line is the score, which is a weighted sum of the values of the gates.

Because he wanted to meet a woman who shared at least some of his interests and passions—which include golfing, playing the flute, watching the Sharks hockey team, eating sushi, and exploring his spiritual side—Tom also searched the profiles for the following key words, "golf," "spirit" (to find the words "spirit" and "spiritual"), "flute," "sharks," and "sushi." He listed those words at the end of the line if he found them in a profile. Tom is now happily involved in a relationship with Mary, one of the women he met online. You can read about Mary and about their relationship on pages 129 and 160.

Chapter 7

Learning E-Mail Etiquette

E-mail etiquette is particularly important in online dating because the recipients of your messages can't see your facial expressions or hear the tone of your voice. This chapter describes good manners for e-mail correspondence. Your words can be misinterpreted if you aren't careful; for example, a joke might be perceived as an insult.

Subject Lines

Give your message a subject line that will indicate to the recipient what your message is about. A subject line in the header of an e-mail message starts with the words "Subject" followed by a colon; for example, "Subject: Want to meet for coffee?" Some people look at the subject line to decide whether to read a message. Assist them, as well as people who may like to store and then later retrieve your message, by indicating the subject matter in the subject field.

When you reply, most e-mail software inserts "Re:" before the subject line of the original message. Change the subject line if it isn't relevant to what you're sending.

Replies

Check your e-mail and reply to it regularly, even if you have time only to acknowledge that you received the message. Many people just ignore messages that don't pique their interest. Several women and men have told me that they consider people rude who do not acknowledge their e-mail.

Many people—mainly women—don't respond to e-mail from people they find uninteresting. If you sent e-mail and haven't received a response, you don't know whether the addressee is on vacation, is busy with other things, has mistakenly deleted your message, didn't read your message, is giving you the cold shoulder, or is not sure what to write back.

Show appreciation for someone who took an interest in you. Be considerate and acknowledge e-mail from people who respond to your ad. If you want to learn more, send a message with questions. Respond to e-mail even to say that you're not interested in corresponding. One of the people you reject may introduce you to your mate. I told Kate, a friend of mine, about Matthew, who told me that he didn't feel compatible with me. They're now getting along well.

How long does it take to send a short message? Take half a minute to acknowledge receipt, even if only to express lack of interest. If you don't want to take the time to respond to messages you receive, develop form letters that you can send out easily and quickly.

- If you don't have time to write a full response to a message, at least acknowledge that you received it, and give the sender a time frame with which you'll get back to him.

```
Just wanted to let you know I got your
message.  I don't have time to write
back right now.  I'll write you more
in a couple of days.  If you don't hear
```

```
from me within the next week, feel free
to drop me a note.
```

- If you feel inundated with responses, say something like:

```
Thanks for your e-mail.  I appreciate
your writing to me.  I'm simply unable
to reply promptly and fully to all responses
to my ad.  But I want you to know that
I did receive your e-mail and read it.
I'll check out your profile and will
write back to you if I think we're likely
to make a good match.
```

- If you are not interested, tell how you feel.

```
Thanks for writing to me.  I checked
out your profile and I don't think we
would be a good match.  Best wishes
in your search.
```

Reply promptly. I've met plenty of people who have forgotten about a message after a few days. It just got lost in their inbox.

When quoting another person, responding to a question, or discussing a point raised in an e-mail message or profile, edit out whatever isn't directly applicable to your reply. Include enough of the message or profile so the recipient can figure out what you're writing about. Also provide a visual indication that distinguishes your comments from the original source material. Some e-mailers do this automatically. One common convention is to precede lines from the original message with an angle brace, >. For example,

```
> Wear sunscreen.

Thanks for the advice.
```

Style Guidelines

Make your message easy for the recipient to read. Not all e-mail programs break lines at word boundaries. So strive to make your lines fit on most computer screens by keeping your line length under seventy characters. Avoid use of bold-face, italics, or control keys because they aren't treated uniformly across systems.

Here's more advice on style from *The Net: User Guidelines and Netiquette* by Arlene Rinaldi, which can be found on the Web at http://www.fau.edu/rinaldi/net/elec.html.

- Capitalize words only to highlight an important point or to distinguish a title or heading. Capitalizing whole words that are not titles is generally interpreted as SHOUTING!

- *Asterisks* surrounding a word can be used to make a stronger point, the way italics are used in print.

- Use the underscore symbol before and after something you wish to underline, such as the title of a book: _Putting Your Heart Online_.

Message Content

Carefully consider what you're willing to disclose to other people; remember, the recipient may forward your e-mail.

Treat the security of e-mail messages about the same as messages on postcards: Recognize that anyone along the chain of distribution can see what you have said, and other people may peek too. If your message contains sensitive material, encrypt your message (using an encryption program such as PGP, which I describe in Appendix A on page 171), or use another, more secure, form of transmission.

Be careful how you express yourself, so that you don't inadvertently convey the wrong impression. Be especially careful when you're using sarcasm and humor. Without seeing your facial expressions or hearing your tone of voice, other people may view your joke as serious criticism. If you mean to say something in jest, use a *smiley:* :-) (tilt your head to the left to see the smiling face). Other smileys or emoticons are listed in the Appendix on page 208. Strive to be clear. It's better to err on the side of spelling out your intended meaning clearly than to be misunderstood.

Basic Rules

- Be tolerant of people's ignorance and mistakes. Some people are new to electronic communication and may be poor typists or bad spellers, or they may accidentally delete your message and ask you to send it again.

- Don't pretend you're someone else when sending e-mail.

- Unless you want to appear sexist, abusive, or bigoted, avoid sending sexist, abusive, harassing, threatening, or bigoted messages.

- Don't launch into a tirade about your former lovers.

- Be cautious about giving out your last name, your address, or other information that might identify you to someone you don't yet know.

Advice (mainly) for Men

In *The Straight FAQ*, Dean Esmay advises:

- *Don't* push to get her telephone number. *Don't* push for a face to face meeting. *Don't* whine to her about your personal problems with women. *Don't* talk about sex (or anything of that nature).

Instead, be friendly and be polite. Ask her about herself, and tell a bit more about yourself. Ask her questions. Encourage her to ask you about anything she might be curious about. Find out about her without being nosy—don't ask for her address, or where she works (but asking what town she lives in is probably okay).

- *Don't* pester her with lots of e-mail. Let her explore who you are at her own pace. If she takes a couple of days to respond to one of your letters, sit on your fingers and *wait*. If it's been more than three or four days, you might try *one* letter to the effect of "Hey, where'd you go?" but that's *it*. If you don't hear anything more, either she doesn't want to talk to you, or she's not reading her e-mail anymore, or she's just busy.

  Keep this in mind: it's scary for a woman to go away for a few days and to come back and find a dozen plaintive, "Oh where, oh where, did you go?" letters. It just makes you look desperate and weird.

- All in all, the most important thing to remember in this situation is that it is *easy to scare a woman away*. If she thinks you're a weirdo, or a psychotic, or a pathetic, lonely loser, she's going to walk away. (And by the way, if you act like a pathetic, lonely loser, *stop it*. Find something else to do with your time and realize that the only way you're going to get a woman is if you stop assuming you'll never get one.)

Advice (mainly) for Women

Here's advice for women.

- Don't complain or send jokes about how horrible men are.

- Sexism is sexism and bigotry is bigotry, even if it's a woman being sexist or bigoted.

- Answer your e-mail, even if only to say, "Thanks for your message. I'm not interested. Best wishes."

E-Mail Providers

If you're using someone else's or your employer's computer, be careful what you say over e-mail; other people might see your message. If you would rather that they not be able to see your e-mail, consider storing your e-mail on another computer, at an Internet Service Provider (ISP), commercial online service (COS), or a free e-mail service. See page 166 of Appendix A for how to find an ISP or COS.

Using an e-mail forwarding service, you can deliver your incoming e-mail to multiple accounts and accept or reject your incoming e-mail based on defined criteria. Bigfoot is one such service. Using Bigfoot, you can set up a free e-mail account using whatever name you want—*YourName*@bigfoot.com.

If you want to keep your personal e-mail off the computer on which you work, consider using a free online e-mail service that stores your e-mail on its site. Using a free online e-mail service makes sense if you're using your employer's (or ex-lover's) computer, because the owner of the computer can open files. Several companies offer free e-mail services, including:

Hotmail	www.hotmail.com
Juno	www.juno.com
RocketMail	www.rocketmail.com
Yahoo!	www.yahoo.com

Check It Over

Read your message carefully before you send it. Run it through
a spell checker. Correct your mistakes. Once you send it, there's
no way to unsend it.

Remember, you're communicating with a person—not with
a computer, e-mail program, or text editor. Unlike computers,
people have feelings and interpret what they read. Think about
how the words you use might be construed when read by someone
who doesn't know you. Also think about what you're willing to
have seen by people other than the recipient.

Chapter 8

Responding to Ads

Many men have complained that they often get no response from the women to whom they write. In this chapter, I offer advice on what to write to elicit responses to your e-mail. I include sample e-mail messages, both alluring and uninviting.

Sample Messages

Suppose that you meet someone at a party. What impression would you create if you introduce yourself and strike up a conversation by saying, "Hi. I find you attractive. I've put information about myself on the bulletin board on the other side of the room. Please take a look at it and let me know if you want to chat."? That's essentially what you're doing when you send messages like these:

```
I was intrigued by your profile.  Rather
than leave a long description here, I'll
refer you to my listing under "TallAndDark"
for more details.  Please check me out,
and if you think I'm worth exploring, I
hope you'll get in touch.  I look forward
to hearing from you!
```

or

> You sound like a sweet person from your
> profile. Would you check out mine and
> see whether you think we might be compatible?

Although I don't recommend sending messages like these, the
last one was a success. Mark sent that message to Florence; she
thought it was a form letter, but nevertheless she checked out his
profile and wrote back to him. Now they are married.

These messages put the recipient on the spot. They force
her to work—to look at your profile and to see whether she finds
anything of interest in it. I suggest that you provide relevant
information. Instead of making her log in to the matchmaking
service to see your ad, include your profile in your e-mail to her.

What if you said, "You (or your ad) caught my eye. Let me
tell you a bit about me...," then proceeded to tell her about your
interests, hobbies, and life goals? That might not work either;
you might come across as arrogant or self-centered. This message
is generic. There is no sign that the author read the ad to which
he is responding. Maybe the author sent this message to every
single woman on the service. Make sure to include something
about the ad that triggered your response. Give her a reason
to think that you're worth her time. Ask her questions to show
your interest and to encourage a response. Engage her.

> To: OneForMe
> From: Ryan@heartsonline.com
> Subject: I'm intrigued
>
>
> I just looked you over--I mean, I looked
> over your profile. I love it for several
> reasons. Wit and intelligence turn me
> on. I share your interest in backpacking,
> rollerblading, and fine dining. In addition,

> you're a neighbor! Out of curiosity, what
> are your favorite cafes and restaurants
> in the area?
>
> I look forward to hearing from you soon.
>
> Ryan

Here's a strange provocative message I received:

> News flash! Bay Area is experiencing a
> major shortage in shoes. You are allowed
> to keep but one pair. Which one pair would
> it be, and why?

I found it easy to come up with a response to this note:

> That's easy! The ones that I'm wearing
> right now. They are made by Ecco. I just
> noticed that they are made in Portugal.
> Last night I went to a costume party and
> I was wearing heels, but after walking
> down to the car, I changed into my Ecco's.
> So instead of looking flashy, I was comfortable.
> I sometimes wear my Eccos when I bicycle.

I decided to ask an equally provocative question:

> If you knew you were going to die tomorrow,
> what would you do today, assuming that
> you would be physically capable of doing
> anything you chose?

He said he would "fly into the Sun. It would be an incredible experience, particularly if I wasn't going to die."

Play with the other person's ad. Put humor in your response. How would you respond to this ad that Florence wrote for her good friend Elaine?

```
Hi there, I'm a mature redhead in the San
Francisco Bay Area. My qualities?  Shy
& seductive, sophisticated & silly, spicy
& sweet, surprising & steady, sunny & stormy,
subtle & salacious, submissive & shameless,
sly & straightforward, a real serene spitfire.
If you want to know about the rest of the
alphabet, you'll just have to ask!
```

Since this ad was filled with words that begin with the letter 'S' and the author alluded to the alphabet, Richard concluded his response with the question, "Would you like to get together for T?"

When to Write

Should you respond to an ad immediately? Is the online dating scene like the housing market in San Francisco: If you don't act quickly, you lose the opportunity?

If you're not hearing back from the people to whom you write, try responding the moment that you spot someone who interests you. Be the first. People are more likely to respond to their first prospect than to their seventeenth. Alternatively, you could wait a few weeks after someone has signed up, then write to her when she is no longer the newest hot thing on the service. Such a strategy can be risky because some people may not remain on the service for long.

What to Write

Words are the most important commodity in the online environment. There is no body language, inflection, pauses, subtle tones of voice, or eye contact. You have to convey your message through text and formatting.

You're writing to get attention. You should target your writing to a specific individual. Much of the advice on writing an ad in Chapter 5, also applies to writing a response:

- Be honest, but don't be confessional.

- Show enthusiasm for aspects of her ad that caught your attention. As you might in a conversation, respond to points mentioned in the ad with comments and questions.

- Give compliments freely, but sincerely.

- Be witty, interesting, creative, and pleasant, both in the subject line and in your message.

- Show intelligence or, at least, a lack of sloppiness: write in complete sentences and check your spelling and grammar.

- Choose your words and content carefully. Avoid obscure jargon. If someone doesn't understand what you're talking about, chances are he won't be impressed.

- Share personal information about yourself. Make your personality and character shine through. Let the recipient know that you're a real person worth meeting. If the person doesn't find you interesting, better to know sooner than later.

- Minimize descriptions of your physical characteristics, even if you are good looking. It's so easy for anyone to say that she is incredibly attractive, regardless of whether she is. Also, beauty is in the eye of the beholder. So why should the recipient believe what you say you look like? Better to send a photograph.

- Become a good storyteller.

- Put in a hook—ask an open-ended question.

- Copy your profile into your e-mail so the recipient doesn't have to search for it.

Here are things to avoid:

- Don't whine.
- Don't just make a list of your selling points; weave them into the e-mail.
- Don't tell everything about yourself. Leave the person wanting to know more.

How to Start a Conversation

If you met someone in person, you might say, "That's a nice shirt. Out of curiosity, where did you buy it?" A similar approach works well via e-mail when you comment on someone's interests or hobbies. For example, you could say, "Your ad piqued my interest." Then, make a friendly positive comment about the content, and follow up with a question: "I was pleased that we have several interests in common, including playing squash, bicycling, and watching documentary films. How did you get started in squash? Where do you play?"

Here are tips for starting a conversation:

- Find common ground.
- Refer to the topics of the day. Read magazines, books, newspapers, and the Web; stay up to date on current events and topics.
- Respond and write in a straightforward, confident manner.
- Express your opinions.
- End most of your remarks with a question to maintain the conversation.

- Ask open-ended questions, whose answers will reveal something about the person.

    - How did you pick your handle? What is its significance?
    - Why did you move here?
    - How do you like your neighborhood?
    - Where would you like to live if you could live anywhere?
    - What do you like to do on your vacations?
    - How was your day?
    - What would you consider an ideal first date?
    - What books or magazines are on your night stand?
    - What are your favorite movies, TV shows, plays, performances, or books?
    - What do you enjoy doing in your free time?
    - What is your profession?

Some people have difficulty answering questions that are open-ended and not specific, such as:

    - What's new?
    - Would you tell me about yourself?
    - What have you been up to lately?

Don't ask closed-ended questions, which have only a factual answer; they don't give the person an opportunity to reveal his personality. Here are closed-ended questions:

    - What degrees do you have?
    - Do you like the beach?
    - What's your favorite color?
    - Do you have any sisters or brothers?
    - Are your parents alive?

What Not to Ask

While Fred, whose profile is shown on page 48, was on a business trip, Teresa sent a long and energetic note to him. After he returned, he sent Teresa a short note letting her know that he was back in town and had received her note. Teresa sent another long note in which she shared details about herself and her interests. She seemed happy to hear from him and interested in getting to know him. She told that she had recently changed jobs and was now ready to get into a relationship.

It was late at night when Fred finally got around to reading Teresa's e-mail. He didn't feel up to writing a long reply, but wanted to let Teresa know that he was interested in conversing. So Fred wrote a short message saying he was glad that they had connected and he would send along a longer note soon. "Short nice message," Fred thought.

Wanting to know in advance whether he would find Teresa attractive, at the end of the note, Fred asked if she had a picture she could send him. He had found that, regardless of whether he initiated or responded to women, many requested his photograph. Fred assumed that requesting one was pro forma for interacting with people online.

The following day, Fred got an angry letter back from Teresa in which she told him that she pondered all day about how to respond to his request for her photo because she was offended that he was more interested in her looks than in her mind. She closed by saying that she had no interest in interacting with him any more.

Fred was shocked by Teresa's response, but consoled himself by thinking that it was better to know about her attitude sooner than later. Fred sent a note back thanking Teresa for sharing her thoughts. He mentioned that many women had requested his picture, which gave him the idea of asking for hers.

Fred thought over this experience to determine whether there was any way he could have foreseen Teresa's reaction. He couldn't think of anything that would have indicated to him that she would be upset. After contemplation, he decided to revise his profile to include the word "open-minded" to the list of attributes he was looking for in a woman. He already had witty, good conversationalist in the list. He hopes that women will read his ad carefully and pay attention to his desires. The moral of this story is: *Go slow, and be careful what you say. One tiny insensitive or misinterpreted remark can cause someone to take offense.*

You may mar your prospects if you start a conversation with these questions:

- Would you please send me your photograph?
- What are you wearing?
- What do you look like?
- What is your telephone number?

Women tend to find such questions distasteful. Some people, typically women, find it scary to give out their telephone numbers. For a better way to get someone's telephone number, see page 149.

A poor conversationalist might make these errors:

- Open with a negative comment; for example, "I hate e-mail. It's so slow."
- Ask personal questions too directly and too soon—"When did you lose your virginity?"
- Make the interaction sound like an interview; "Please tell me what you've done in your life and why I would want to spend time with you."

Be aware that you are being judged not only by your ad, but also by your e-mail.

How to use E-Mail

In your e-mail, you want to write about why an ad appeals to you, particularly if you're initiating contact. It's also best to give your first name. There's no reason to send a long letter with the story of your life to a total stranger. Instead, keep your note short, and put in basic information to catch her interest. This first letter is the hook. Less is more. Save the rest for when you receive a response. Here's a possible letter, which is a response to the ad listed on page 59:

> Subject: *Start with a witty heading or a reference to her profile:* I'm also seeking a monogamous, intimate relationship
>
> Hi *name or handle,*
>
> While I was online the other night, I searched for single women who live near me and I came across your profile. *Comment on something in her ad that caught your eye.* And you certainly don't look your age in your photo! *Give a brief description of yourself.* Do I fit your "want list"? I do not have a perfect score. I certainly have a number of your preferred qualities. I should score high on your emotion/passion scale: I've gotten good reviews in the past from exes. I'm adventurous, well-educated (Columbia University grad, and, just recently, about 2 years toward an MFA), and moderately well-traveled. I'm not married (any more), don't "have a thing for my ex" (though we're still friendly). I'm smart and funny

and honest and never intentionally mean.
*Feel free to reveal some of your negative
points.* And now the "financially secure"
part. Hmmmmmm. I always wonder exactly
what that means. It seems to range from
(1) "Is rich," through (2) "Owns home and
can support a free-spending wife," down
to (3) "Can periodically eat out and won't
ask to borrow rent money." In my case,
I'm nowhere near 1 or 2, but I am a ways
above 3, even now. It's through a combination
of doing what I wanted rather than what
paid well (i.e., publishing), plus divorce,
plus a couple of years in grad school,
plus trying to make it in a new career
this year. Thus, I *do* have a balance
on my credit card at the moment, for the
first time in my life. If I can continue
to get work of the sort I've got now, it
should be gone by Christmas.
        Soooooo ... now that you know my (not
too) dark side ... I have been warned
that you're picky ... just be honest (but
tactful)·....
        Ask a few open-ended questions. What
do you enjoy most about traveling abroad?
When, where, and why were you last abroad?

The online matchmaking service reported that David and I
lived two miles apart. Here's the first e-mail message I received
from David:

Hi. I read somewhere that the best indicator
that a relationship will work out is that
you live within ten minutes of each other.

> I don't put much stock in that, really.
> But it does make it easier to get to know
> each other.
>   I'm financially secure. I honestly
> have most of my dreams. What I'm missing
> is someone to share them with, so that's
> what I'm working on turning into reality.
> Thus this letter. Read my profile, write,
> let me know what you think.
>   What are your degrees in? What area
> do you live in? I live on the north side
> of the UCB campus, very near to the campus,
> in a great apartment with a wonderful view
> of the bay.

I was pleased with his response and his profile, I wrote back immediately.

What If You're at a Loss What to Write

If you can't figure out what to write, there are Web sites to help you. The Cyrano Server, at `http://www.nando.net/toys/cyrano`, is one such site. Cyrano will help you to write valentines, love letters, and break-up notices. The Cyrano server is a bit like Mad Libs, a game I used to play when I was a child.

For the love letter, you provide a style (steamy, indecisive, surreal, desperate, intellectual, poetic, or regretful); your name; a few adjectives, nouns, and adverbs; an attractive physical feature; a garment; and your beloved's name. Cyrano composes a letter for you.

How Many People to Contact

Respond to several ads at a time to increase your chances of connecting with someone. Not everyone will reply. Meeting people will help you to build your confidence. It will also help you learn who you are, what you desire, and what you can't tolerate. Remember, if you have high standards, you may have to meet lots of people to find someone who's right for you. But don't write to more people than you can handle if they all respond. I find that my maximum is half a dozen people at a time. Focus on writing high-quality messages, rather than on churning out a large quantity.

If you're a woman, respond to ads. You might be surprised at the positive reaction that you receive when you take the initiative.

Chapter 9

Succeeding with E-Mail

The dynamics of e-mail relationships are different from those of telephone and face-to-face relationships. You probably wouldn't call someone half a dozen times in one day, but many people send each other half a dozen e-mail messages per day. People tend to reveal more about themselves and have more intense interactions with new acquaintances they meet over the Internet than with people they meet at a singles event or through a dating service. If you don't know someone's address, you can't send flowers or greeting cards, but you can send virtual flowers and Internet valentines. If someone asks you a question on the telephone, it can be difficult or awkward not to answer it. On e-mail, it is easier to avoid or defer responding. E-mail is less intrusive than the telephone; you can read and respond to it at your convenience.

E-Mail Stories

Some amusing situations can result when people correspond anonymously.

Too Close for Comfort

Tina received e-mail from a man named Greg who saw her ad online. They started corresponding. He told her quite a bit about himself, including the names and ages of his children. She knew he lived close to her, because the online service had indicated that they were three miles apart. After a few e-mail messages, Tina figured out that she knew Greg: They were good buddies at work! They had even carpooled together for a while. Until she figured out that she knew him, she wasn't aware that he had been looking to meet a woman; he was a private person. She felt strange knowing some of his personal feelings that he hadn't previously revealed to her.

She didn't know what to do. She no longer felt enthusiastic about sending him e-mail. Should she let him know her true identity and see what he wanted to do? Alternatively should she tell him enough about herself that he would figure out who she was? She had mixed feelings about both these strategies; either could lead to an awkward situation. She and Greg worked together and were close professionally; they talked to each other about technical matters all the time. What if they did start seeing each other romantically and it didn't work out?

Feeling uncomfortable, she stopped writing to Greg. Later she found out from Jennifer—the woman who had introduced both of them to online dating—that Greg discontinued his membership on the matchmaking service because he "just isn't ready to meet strangers." I would have advised Tina to let Greg know that she didn't wish to pursue their relationship.

Why Now and Not Back Then?

Carl and Tracy met each other online. They corresponded for about one month before meeting face to face. Within three months of that first meeting, they decided to get married. A few months after they moved in with each other, Carl showed

Tracy the correspondence that he had had with several women over a few years online. Tracy was surprised to see that one of the messages was from her. She had written "Thanks for writing to me. I checked out your profile and I don't think we would make a great match. Best wishes in your search." They are getting along so well now that Tracy wonders why she didn't see any possibility two years earlier, particularly since they are trying to have children now and it might have been better to start a couple of years earlier. The moral of this story is: *Don't reject a person too quickly. He might be much more interesting than he first appears.*

Responding to E-Mail

"I just heard back from `NewToTheArea`! What should I do?" asks Jim. "Should I write back right away to show I'm interested? Should I play it cool and sit on it for several days?" Dean Esmay offers great advice in *The Straight FAQ*:

> Q. *She wrote me, she wrote me, she wrote me!! Omigod what do I do?*
>
> A. Simmer down. All the lady did was decide your ad was interesting and send you e-mail. She's not ready to jump into your arms and have your baby. She's just given you a nibble. Remember, if this doesn't work out, there *will* be other women, if you have a good ad and are just patient!
>
> Here are important things to keep in mind:
>
> Don't question it: She *is* interested in you, or she wouldn't have answered your ad. So, get over your insecurities. She's a woman looking for a man, and you sound interesting to her. Now you just have to see whether you're interested in her, and whether there's

enough of what she wants in you to sustain her interest.

Here's my advice:

- Keep the momentum going when you get a response. If someone expresses interest, don't hesitate. Write back within twenty-four hours. Be aware that ignoring a person can cause pain and annoyance. If he doesn't hear back from you, he may find someone else to take your place. Show respect. Respond to e-mail even just to say that you aren't interested.

- Reply to people who seem not to be your perfect match. Something good may happen anyway if you're open to it, or they may introduce you to their friends.

- When you're asked closed-ended questions, try to answer more than the question at hand. Elaborate.

- Make the person feel good. Give compliments generously about their characteristics that you truly like. But don't go overboard, or you may sound insincere.

- Make an effort to share information about yourself and to listen to what the other person has to say.

- Look for what you share in common.

- Reveal appropriate facts about yourself without demanding the same from the other person.

- What if someone asks you a question you don't care to answer, such as, "Why did you and your wife get divorced?" Some people prefer not to talk about their troubles—at least not just when they're getting to know someone. You could say, "We went our separate ways." What if the person asks, "No, what really happened?" One possible response would be, "I don't feel comfortable discussing that now. When we know each other better, I'll tell you more about it." This response shows that you have tact and are honest.

- Don't take it personally if you don't receive a response. People reject other people for the flimsiest reasons, or they may no longer be looking.

- If you want to know where you stand with someone, ask her.

Flirting over Your Modem

How do you flirt online?

- Respond promptly to e-mail.

- Chat in a conversational manner.

- Share your feelings and personal information about yourself.

- Compliment the other person.

- Tell jokes or amusing stories, followed by the *emoticon* :-) to indicate that what you are saying is intended to be funny.

- Send several messages per day.

- Give someone virtual flowers, virtual kisses, greeting cards, or postcards via the Internet.[1] In my profile, I mentioned that I speak French. One clever man sent me a virtual postcard in French from Digital Dream. Some people like to receive a note or greeting card; other people would rather receive a message that you created yourself.

---

[1]Internet postcards are offered on several sites including: www.marlo.com www.digitaldream.com, and postcards.www.media.mit.edu/Postcards.

Moving to Real E-Mail and Real Names

When do you exchange real e-mail addresses and real names?
When you feel comfortable. Some people have no qualms about
giving out their real names and e-mail addresses. Other people
don't want to put themselves in a vulnerable situation; they want
to minimize the chances of being stalked or harassed.

Martha is cautious about giving out her real name. The
earliest she has given it out is in her third e-mail. She never
reveals it in the first or second e-mail. "I want to know a man is
who he says he is before I give him my name. I also want to feel
that I have a relationship prospect before I reveal my name."

Exchanging Photographs

As digital images become commonplace, more people are exchanging photographs. But not everyone is comfortable showing
a photograph:

- They don't want people to recognize them. (Although it
  can be difficult to recognize someone from a small online
  photograph.)

- They want you to get to know them by their words rather
  than by their looks. Both attractive and unattractive people feel this way.

- They don't have good pictures (or scans) of themselves.

- They don't consider themselves attractive.

- They don't know how to send a photograph through the
  Internet and they don't want to admit their ignorance of
  technology. See Appendix A on page 169 for instructions
  on how to e-mail a photograph.

- They want to see your reaction to their looks when you first meet.

- They don't want you to be able to forward their photographs to someone else.

It's best not to start your message by asking for a photograph. You may appear shallow. Appear to care more about his personality than about his looks!

When should you exchange photographs? When you are ready, why not send your photograph before asking someone to send hers? I have known men to offer to send their photographs if I sent mine. They want to create an incentive for women to write to them.

What if someone is reluctant to send her photograph—does that mean she's unattractive? No. Beautiful people get plenty of attention. They might like people to judge them by what's inside, rather than by their appearance.

Understanding E-Mail Dynamics

People tend to write e-mail as they would talk to each other. E-mail interaction is halfway between a telephone conversation and an exchange of letters. Like the recipient of a letter, the recipient of e-mail can't read the message when you're composing it. Also like a letter, the message originates from one person; but unlike a letter, e-mail is delivered almost instantaneously when you send it, regardless of whether the destination is next door or halfway around the world. People often send and receive several messages a day to and from one person: they are having a conversation. But unlike long-distance telephone calls, even long-distance e-mail interactions usually are free or nearly so.

Some people check their e-mail several times per week; other people check it several times per day. Some people spend as much as several hours per day reading and responding to e-mail.

People tend to ask and reveal more personal information to new acquaintances over e-mail than they do on the telephone or in person. For example, some people will ask, "Have you ever been married?" in e-mail when they wouldn't think of doing so in a telephone conversation; or, a woman will write directly that she is not interested in going out with a man, but she'll make up an excuse if he asks her out over the telephone. With e-mail, you have more time to reflect on what to say and how to say it.

Some people read more into a message than the author intended to convey. In real life, a person can say something stupid. Fortunately, there is no way to turn back time and hear the stupid statement again; some careless remarks are quickly forgotten. That's not the case with e-mail; be careful what you write.

A Voluminous Romance

Can you fall in love with someone whom you haven't met face to face? I'll share a personal story that will address that question.

One day, I received e-mail from a guy named Jacob who lived in Chicago. We started an intense correspondence. Every morning, I would wake up to find a message or two from him. We exchanged about a dozen messages daily. He told me about his passion for scuba diving and gourmet cooking. I recounted my obsession for squash (the racquet game) and my love of film festivals. We described how we keep physically active and what our current business projects were. We wrote about our neighborhoods, our experiences traveling abroad, our families, our jobs, our desires, and our day-to-day activities. Although we had never seen each other face to face, I felt at ease sharing intimate details with him.

I checked out Jacob's Web page. It had a description of his work projects and a long list of publications. There was no personal information, but there was a formal photograph of him. I was pleased with his appearance.

I was falling in love online! I told my friends and family about Jacob. My mother told me about having corresponded with my father after they met during a trip my father made to California from Washington, D.C., to interview with several companies. Many of my friends were happy that I had met a man. A few friends seemed surprised that I was so taken by someone whom I hadn't met in person.

Jacob considered taking a business trip to California, but because he had many other commitments, he decided against it. I was planning a trip to Poland that summer and he was going to France around the same time. We considered a rendezvous in London or in Paris. Jacob wrote:

```
If we get along, I can't think of a more
romantic place to meet.  Just think of
all the wonderful places we can eat.  And
when people ask us where we met, it would
be fun to say "at Charles DeGaulle Airport
in Paris."
```

A couple of days later, Jacob chickened out and instead invited me to drop by Chicago on my way to Poland. I decided to stay in a hotel not far from Jacob's apartment.

During my flight to Chicago, I read through all the e-mail I'd received from Jacob. After arriving at O'Hare Airport, I took a shuttle to my hotel. During the ride, I imagined us chatting a mile a minute over dinner. I called Jacob once I arrived at my hotel to let him know that I was ready for dinner. He came over about ten minutes later.

Conversation was more awkward than I would have expected, considering that we had exchanged hundreds of pages of e-mail over the past month. It was also one-sided. After five hours of conversation, he didn't know anything about my travel plans, the reason for my trip to Poland, or my age. I, on the other hand, was intimately acquainted with his reasons for accepting a position in Chicago, the layout of his office, the location of his cubicle, his importance to his company, and the meeting he had with an investor earlier that day. The questions he asked showed that he didn't remember the facts that I had shared with him in my e-mail. I, on the other hand, could recite details about his life that he had shared with me, because I had reread our correspondence at least a half dozen times, most recently on the airplane.

Jacob was a great writer. Somehow I had missed the fact that his voluminous e-mail had not been responsive to mine. He didn't seem interested in anything I talked about; his focus was on the next thing that he wanted to say. He would pick out one kernel of information from what I said and use it to launch into something about himself or his life. Not feeling appreciated, I didn't want to be with him—I had no desire to see him again.

The moral of this story is: *Try not to get swept off your feet by e-mail. Talk over the telephone before you develop firm impressions.*

E-Mail Romances

E-mail romances run a course slightly different from their physical world counterparts. People learn about each other's personalities and writing abilities before they find out whether there's physical attraction. They share their thoughts, hopes, dreams, and interests; they say what's going on in their lives. They become more intimate, sharing more details about themselves at an earlier stage in their relationship, than would a couple who first met in the physical world.

Online, you don't have to worry about how you look, where you're going, how you're getting there, and who will pay the bill. You have time to contemplate what the other person wrote, and to reflect on how to respond. Some people let their imaginations run wild. They feel a close connection. They fall in love with the image they have created, rather than with the person who sends them e-mail. Are they in love? No, they are attracted to a person's writing style, his way of expressing himself, and perhaps his photograph. There is a lot they don't know about the person. There's a good chance that their relationship will fall apart after they talk on the telephone or meet in person.

Does that mean you shouldn't bother meeting people in cyberspace? Not at all. Just don't let your imagination get carried away before talking on the telephone or meeting in person.

The Internet is one way to meet people. Unless you desire an Internet-only relationship, take steps to move to the physical world as soon as you feel ready.

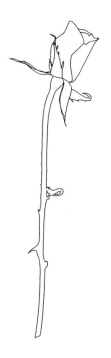

Part III

Beyond the Net

Myth: It happens when you're not looking.

No! That's when you bump into a wall.

When asked what they regret most in their lives, many older people say they wish they had taken more risks. When you are looking back on your life, would you rather think about the opportunities that you missed or about all the wonderful (or terrible!) experiences that you had?

Chapter 10

Exchanging Information

Would you buy a new TV without examining its features? Would you accept a job without finding out the salary? Probably not, because you wouldn't want to make a mistake. Similarly, collect information before you get involved with someone so you can be sure that you aren't getting close to the wrong person. Get to know that someone by asking questions and by seeing how she conducts herself.

This chapter suggests questions to ask and techniques for finding information about a person. It also provides methods that can be helpful in deciding whether this person suits you and whether the two of you in the long term will enjoy each other's company.

Don't Make Assumptions

Have you heard the story about the engineer, the statistician, and the lawyer who were riding together on a train through the countryside when they noticed a flock of sheep? The engineer noted that practically all the sheep were white. The statistician observed that just one sheep out of the flock of thirty-six was black. The lawyer cautiously said the side visible from the train was white on all of the sheep but one, on which it was black.

Notice that the lawyer drew no conclusions beyond what she could see. Similarly, you shouldn't draw any conclusions about someone based on e-mail, on a conversation on the telephone, or a meeting. Check someone out before you get involved.

Is the Person Available?

After corresponding with George for about a week, I decided to call him. We started off by saying hello and exchanging a few pleasantries. George encouraged me to ask him anything. At the time, I had just started to write this chapter and I had put together a list of questions. First on my list was, "Are you single?" Figuring that most people on a matchmaking service were available, I almost didn't ask it, but I'm glad that I did because it turned out George was separated and hadn't yet filed for a divorce. To me, that means he's not single. I wasn't interested in meeting a man who could not marry whenever he wants to; I don't want to have to go through the emotional fallout of a divorce or the possibility of his reconciliation with his wife. The moral of this story is: *Don't assume that people are single just because they are using an online matchmaking service.* Be aware that some people will lie, or will not tell the complete truth.

When you meet someone, don't wait too long before asking what might seem like obvious questions.

- Are you single?
- Are you getting over someone else?
- Are you truly emotionally available?

Why waste time if a person isn't legally or emotionally available, if you want someone who is?

Ask About these Aspects

For what qualities are you looking in a mate? What did you put on your list in the exercise on page 37? Are you seeking someone who has a Porsche, a private plane, nice eyes, a great body? Someone who shares your interest in skiing and sailing? How important is it that your partner be honest and feel good about himself? Instead of asking someone about his vacation plans, car, eye, or hair color, consider finding out about his

- Availability (is he open to being involved in a relationship?)
- Integrity and maturity (is he responsible and trustworthy?)
- Loyalty (would he be there when you need him?)
- Self-esteem (what is his attitude toward himself and things in his life?)
- Relationships (does he have positive, close relationships with family, friends, and colleagues?)
- Expressiveness and communication skills (does he listen to what you say? does he share his feelings with you?)

Find out about these qualities by asking questions.

Asking Uncomfortable Questions

It's much easier not rocking the boat, by not asking personal questions. But you're making a mistake if you don't. In addition to getting important answers, you find out how the person reacts to personal inquiries and how willing he is to be open about himself. You also discover what his perceptions of himself are and possibly how honest he is.

Consider Will, a literary agent who was interested in representing this book. He faxed me an agreement. If I had just signed it, I wouldn't have learned about how he resolves differences, how he responds when pushed, and how he negotiates. What I learned was he didn't like my approach and had no interest in resolving our differences. So we went our separate ways. Testing a person or your relationship with him early on by asking questions and resolving conflict often will give you a clear indication if there's something worth pursuing.

But be careful not to make the other person feel that he is on a job interview. Don't just fire questions at him; that may turn him off. Figure out how to make him feel comfortable addressing your concerns. Intersperse your inquiries with information about yourself.

It may not be romantic to do a little probing, but it's sensible. If someone's turned off by your cautious nature, better you find that out sooner rather than later.

Relationships

Find out about her relationships with people close to her. How does she feel about them and how does she treat them? Ask questions such as these:

- What was your family like?

- How do you feel about the way your parents raised you?

- How close are you to your siblings?

- Who are your closest friends? What do you do with them?

Learn about a person by seeing whom she chooses as her friends and how they treat her. How do you get along with her friends? How does she get along with yours? What do you think of her friends? What do yours think of her?

Be hesitant about getting involved with someone who fights with her family or her best friends; she may not have a willingness to work out differences and may not show appreciation for people close to her. (But some wonderful people may not have close family ties; don't reject someone just for that reason, unless it's especially important to you.)

Judy said she went out with a man who told her, "both of my ex-wives are suing me." It could be that he married litigious women, but it could be that he isn't fair with his partners. Look for red flags.

How does the person feel about the parent of the opposite sex: How does a man feel about his mother, or how does a woman feel about her father? Those feelings may affect the person's feelings and reactions toward you.

Gail, a friend of mine who has been married twice, advises: "Don't get romantically involved with someone whose family you can't tolerate—no matter how hard you want to believe that your candidate is different. Roots are forever."

You can find out a lot about your potential partner by learning about his previous romantic relationships, as well as his relationship goals. Are his desires in line with yours? Here are a few questions to ask, perhaps not in your first e-mail message, but before you get involved:

- What would be your ideal relationship?
- What are your attitudes toward love, commitment, and communication?
- How much time would you like to spend with your partner?
- Do you have any insecurities about dating and relationships that you are willing to share?

People with similar values tend to stay together. That is why dating services survey your personality when you sign up and try to match you with someone who has similar values. You can find out about someone's values by observing her over time—preferably before you get into a relationship. Do things together, such as shopping, attending parties, and discussing investments. You should be able to learn what her character and lifestyle are like, and what activities she enjoys.

I also recommend that you find out about drinking and drug habits. Remember that a person who drinks heavily may not admit it. You might have to find out some other way; for example, go out for drinks or to a party, and see how he handles his liquor.

Exercise: More Questions to Ask

What information would help you to decide whether to be involved with someone you meet?

1. Review the qualities you want in a mate; look at your answers to the Exercise on page 37. Think of at least ten questions the answers to which will help you to assess whether someone is of interest to you. Here are examples:

   - How did you decide to live where you do?
   - What lifestyle would you like to have?
   - How do you feel about your career and your current job?
   - Of what are you most proud in your life?
   - What are your personal goals?
   - What are your feelings about children?
   - What direction do you see your career taking? What are your professional goals?
   - What do you hope to be doing five years from now?
   - If you could live your life over again, what would you do differently?
   - What do you do when you want to treat yourself well?
   - Do you like risks, or do you avoid them? What major risks have you taken in your life?
   - What are your weaknesses? How do you deal with them?
   - What are your favorite books, TV shows, movies, and music?

- What is your religion? What role does religion play in your life?
- What are the most important aspects of your life?
- If you met your partner through an online dating service, what would you tell your friends and family when they asked where you met?

2. Ethics and Morality. It's also important to learn about a person's ethics and morals. Instead of questioning him directly, consider describing a scenario about a friend, and then asking what he thinks of the situation. Write at least three scenarios. Here are examples:

- Do you think people should drive the speed limit?
- My friend Andy lied about his age in his online profile. How would you feel about a man who lied about his age? What lies do you think are ok in that situation? What lies are not ok?
- John had a one-night stand with Stephanie. He told Carol, his wife, about it. What would you do if you were in Carol's position?
- Williams' 16-year-old daughter, Kerry, accidentally left her diary open on the kitchen table. She had written that she's pregnant and is planning to get an abortion. William read the diary and learned about his daughter's situation. What would you advise that William do?

What Are They Asking About You?

You are judged not only by the answers you give, but also by the questions you ask. If you want to make a favorable impression, think about what you want to know. Your questions convey what is important to you and what your level of commitment to finding a mate is, as well as how well developed your social skills are.

Be cautious with people who ask

- For money
- Intensely personal questions
- For your hand in marriage, particularly before meeting you

Arthur seemed delighted to answer the questions that I asked. He enjoyed having an attentive audience and reflecting on his life. He talked animatedly about himself. However, his asking so few questions raised a red flag. Was he so self-centered that he couldn't think beyond himself? Was he the type of person who might say, "Now that we've talked about me, I'd like to find out a bit about you. What do you think of me?" Or was he simply uninterested in learning anything about me? Was he too shy or insecure to ask? Whatever the reason, I was unimpressed.

What Should You Tell Your Date and When?

Here are some examples of how to reveal and deal with situations that some people consider less than desirable:

- *The two of you live far apart.* If she's worth it, tell her that you'll work it out.

- *You're overweight.* Begin a formal weight-reduction program.

- *You have a serious medical condition (multiple sclerosis).* Maintain a cheerful attitude. Tell prospect at the appropriate time, "My medical condition is a fact. I monitor it and I deal with it. It doesn't rule my life."

- *You hold a low-status job.* Make no excuses. Confidently say, "That's what I do for a living." Develop yourself into an interesting person. If you are rejected because of the work you do, then the person wasn't right for you.

When do you disclose important personal information, emotional baggage, or life-threatening illnesses such as cancer? Mary usually does it on the second date. She feels it's too intense for the first date—and by the third date, fantasies are running wild. Mary explains:

> Cancer is a chronic illness. I hope to have lifelong remission and to die from another cause. But many women die of breast cancer. It's sad but true.

Mary had a lumpectomy. Her breasts don't look like most other women's. She doesn't want to get in a situation where she's taken off her clothes and says, "By the way, I had breast cancer. That's why my breasts may look weird to you."

Mary has told her dates, "I was treated for breast cancer seven years ago." They usually think that she's fine, and they can deal with how she looks. So Mary explains that there is a high risk that at some time the cancer will come back. Most men don't want to know. But she doesn't want to have a recurrence and have her partner turn to her when she's going through a difficult time, and say, "You didn't tell me that this might happen."

Three months after Mary first met Tom, she was diagnosed with recurrent breast cancer. She immediately called him when she heard the news; she said, "This is way beyond anything that you signed up for. I love you and I release you."

Tom didn't leave. He stayed with Mary through her mastectomy. Mary didn't know that she was soon going to have an opportunity to reciprocate: Tom had a heart attack two months after Mary's surgery.

On one of my first dates, when I asked whether Bill was close to his brother, he told me he wasn't and that his brother was in jail for sexually molesting children and soon to be released. Bill informed the community where his brother was planning to live, and out of anger his brother wasn't speaking to him. Bill had decided to speak out to the community because he had regretted

not informing the neighbors about his brother's pedophilia before
he was incarcerated. When I told my good friend Rachel about
this incident, she said this:

> I have been on both sides of this, since I have many
> skeletons in my closet; how do I break it to them—
> three marriages, three divorces, one kid per marriage,
> first marriage to a guy of a different race, and so
> on? Different things turn different people off. Even
> your success and good income can turn some guys off,
> or that you own a home or have a better education.
> Even bad things that happened to you—I had one guy
> freak out when I told him I had been raped. Maybe
> he thought it lessened his chances of getting laid?
> He treated me as if I'd committed a crime—it was
> bizarre. Should there be a "Don't tell unless asked"
> policy? When does it become relevant? Should the
> onus be on the other person to ask enough questions?

I don't know the answers to these questions. I find it hard to
decide whether—or when—to reveal my skeletons. Some men are
accepting of anything. Other men get upset about the smallest
deviation from convention. It tells you a lot about the person if
he can accept you with your skeletons.

If you reveal your skeletons too soon, the other person may
get a distorted perspective of you, since she may know few of your
good points. Here are potential skeletons in people's histories:

- Sexually transmitted disease, such as herpes or AIDS
- Mental illness
- Prison time
- Multiple divorces
- Restraining orders against previous partners or vice versa
- Drug use or abuse (legal, illegal, or prescription)

- Alcohol abuse
- Domestic violence
- Severe credit problems or poverty
- Dishonesty
- Infidelity
- Violence

When a person does reveal a skeleton, find out whether he has changed, grown, or learned from the experience in a positive way. If he has a sexually transmitted disease, is there a way to be sexual safely? Will he go to a doctor with you to find out how you can protect yourself?

What advantages are there to revealing your skeletons?

- Your actions or emotions may not make sense if you hide something that has had a big effect on you.
- The other person will get to know you better.
- If he doesn't accept you with your skeletons, better to find out sooner and move on.

Do Online Background Checking

If you're wary of someone you have met, you might want to do a background verification yourself or through some service. Find out if there's anyone else looking for your newfound love—for example, the police, a creditor, or a spouse. After all, why go after someone who is already wanted?

The Web can assist you in learning about a person's history. Using a search engine, you can look up a person by his name, employer, organizations to which he belongs, or interests. You may find his Web page or references to him on other pages. You can look up a person's handle to see where else it's referenced on the Web. A list of popular search engines is included in the Glossary on page 214.

Deja News (`www.dejanews.com`), which I described in Appendix B, page 182, is another great tool for finding out about someone. Using it, you can find what someone has posted to a discussion group or whether a person has been mentioned in someone else's posting. But be aware that just because Deja News shows you an objectionable remark that a person posted many years ago doesn't necessarily mean that that person still holds the same point of view. What if you run a search and nothing comes up? What does that indicate? That the person has no presence on the Web or on Usenet. It doesn't mean that she hasn't done anything in her life. Run a search on yourself. See what you find, because this information is what other people might uncover about you.

Shortly after Debbie met Steve, she did an AltaVista[1] Web search using his full name and learned he does volunteer work for the California Abortion Rights Action League (CARAL). This information served as a great conversation topic the following evening.

Can you run a search if you don't know someone's last name? Yes. Use the information that you do know. If you know in what company someone works or organizations to which he belongs, you can look on the company or organization's Web page for a man with his first name and who fits his description.

When you look at a Web page, the author is able to collect information about the computer that you use to perform the search. Don't be overly concerned. He can't get your name, telephone number, or address. But he can find the name of the host computer or the name of your Internet Service Provider (ISP), and can see which of his Web pages you accessed, at what time, and what browser you used.

Some people will be delighted that you take an interest in

---

[1]`http://www.altavista.digital.com`

finding out more about them, but be aware that other people might see your research as an invasion of their privacy.

Online Research

This section serves as an illustration of how to use the Net to find important information.

After they had corresponded for several weeks, Ed informed Sara that he had genital herpes. He explained how he had caught the virus from his ex-wife in the early 1980s before people were sensitized to the risk of transmission.

Ed told her that his genital herpes is not contagious except when he has a blistery rash. He tried to put her at ease by explaining that he knows in advance when he is about to have an outbreak and that he only has them about three times a year. He told her that they can refrain from intercourse during those times, or he can use a condom. He told her that the viral infection didn't have much effect on his life, but she suspected that it did. He wasn't pushing to get sexually involved with her, as other men had done.

That night, Sara obsessed about herpes. Lots of questions floated through her mind: How effective would a condom be in protecting her from getting the virus while he was having an outbreak? What is it like to have herpes? Would she have been able to tell that Ed had herpes if he hadn't told her? Would it be possible to catch the virus when Ed was not having an outbreak? How do people who have partners with herpes deal with their situation?

Sara decided to look for answers on the World Wide Web, using Digital's AltaVista search engine. The search netted about 20,000 documents!

She found a page entitled *Coping with Herpes*,[2] which pointed

---

[2]http://www.herpeszone.com/COPE.HTM

to another page entitled *Am I Contagious? When and Where?*[3]
This second page seemed like a good place to start. The article
indicated that about twenty percent of the population carries the
virus: the infection is practically an epidemic. Most people who
harbor the herpesvirus don't know that they do. The article went
on to say

> Studies have indicated that the herpesvirus could wake
> up from its latent or sleeping state and creep silently
> to the skin or mucous membranes without causing
> sores or annoying symptoms. However, the average
> herpes infected individual who suffers from chronic
> recurrent outbreaks can sensitize themselves to the
> patterns that indicate an onset of a herpes outbreak.
> ... Studies have shown that most subclinical shed-
> ding occurred within seven days of a recognized out-
> break. Shedding in the absence of herpes lesions is
> more prevalent with genital herpes.

If this information was correct—and remember that not all postings on the Web are accurate—herpes could be transmitted even
when a person was asymptomatic.

Sara wanted to hear how other people have handled this situation. She ran across a Web page filled with personal and intimate
experiences that people had had with herpes. What she learned
from these personal reports is that the virus affects people more
psychologically than physically.

The moral of this story is: *There is a wealth of information
on the Web.* No longer do you have to go to a library or bookstore
to research a topic. Search engines are powerful tools for learning
about illnesses, as well as about other things. You can find out
about people, places, organizations, books, movies, diseases, and
drugs; you can download maps, and train and plane schedules;

---

[3]`http://www.herpeszone.com/AM_ICONT.HTM`

and you can tap into this tremendous resource from any computer on the Internet. But don't trust everything you read on the Web; anyone can post anything.

Words of Advice

Here are my words of advice on choosing whom to date:

- *Judge a person by his heart, not by his car/house/career.*

- *Don't fall in love with somebody's potential.* Beware of a fixer-upper. Don't expect a person to change. Ask yourself: "Can I love this person the way that he is now?" If you can't, find someone else.

- *Don't fall in love with the wrong person.* Don't overlook red flags out of desperation to have a relationship. Danger signs include abusing substances, monopolizing conversations, and revealing little of himself. If he hasn't fully ended his previous relationship, don't be quick to get involved. If he makes a statement like "I don't do commitment well," believe him! Ask yourself: "Is this person sufficiently available emotionally and situationally to satisfy me?" If someone isn't right, move on.

- *Meet her friends, and have her meet your.* Do you get along with each other's friends?

- *Don't assume your date telepathically knows what you want or need.* Express your thoughts, desires, needs, and feelings.

- *Don't confuse lust with love.* In a rush to feel close, some people have sex prematurely, creating a false sense of intimacy, which can lead to disappointment. Take the time to create a genuine emotional connection and allow a passionate sexual relationship to grow.

I encourage you to consider writing down your first impression of each person whom you contact. After you've gotten to know the person, check whether your first impression was on target. Are you a good judge of character?

Don't get involved too fast. Get to know someone by asking questions and doing your own research. For tips on keeping records on the people whom you contact, see Appendix C.

Chapter 11

Getting Out Gracefully

On the Internet, you can not only meet, but also reject and be rejected. This chapter focuses on the various facets of rejection. It discusses how to recognize when someone is rejecting you or about to reject you; how to overcome fear of rejection and to minimize its pain; how to reject someone, including what to say and whether to do it over the Net, on the telephone, or face to face.

Handling Rejection

Rejection hurts. It's painful for everyone. This section describes how to cope with rejection and to grow from it.

Fear of Rejection and Its Consequences

To find a mate, you may have to meet many people. Much as job interviews improve your skills at interviewing and finding suitable work, dating will help you to get better at finding suitable potential mates. Each date will bring you closer to understanding what you're looking for in a mate, and will make you more comfortable with the process of searching. Therefore, the more experience you have accepting rejection, the easier your search will be.

Don't limit yourself to those people whom you think will accept an invitation from you. If you lower your expectations because you fear rejection, you may be more comfortable in the short term, but in the long term you won't be happy because you won't have what you want and need. More important, you'll be unavailable should the right person come along.

A common technique for dealing with rejection is creative avoidance. That is, you sidestep situations where you might be rejected. For example, you don't approach anyone because you're afraid of being turned down. One of Jenny's friends gave her Larry's telephone number, yet she won't call him. She thinks of all the reasons he might reject her. In so doing, she's missing an opportunity to get to know him and possibly to meet the love of her life (if not Larry, perhaps one of his friends). By avoiding the possibility of rejection, she's also missing opportunities to be chosen.

Do you half-heartedly look for dates because you doubt someone will find you interesting? Do you avoid putting in much effort, thus ensuring the outcome that you anticipate? If so, stop acting as though you deserve people's sympathy. Most people find insecurity and lack of confidence unattractive, even if you are physically beautiful.

Don't let fear of rejection stop you from searching for a partner. Focus on your overall goal, rather than on minor setbacks. One success should be enough. If you get rejected by five people in a row and the sixth wants to go out with you, you're a winner. No one's accepted by everyone. Just think of what it would be like if you were never turned down. Be content that people reject you; if they do, they aren't right for you.

If you don't put yourself in a position where you might be rejected, you're probably missing opportunities to get into a wonderful relationship. Recognize that you limit your rewards if you limit your risk.

Recognizing Rejection

Why don't people just say, "I'm not interested in going out with you?" Wouldn't such a candid, straightforward rejection be easier (and less painful) than its more subtle and indirect variations?

Indirect messages give people a chance to change their mind, not to own up to the rejection, and to avoid confrontation. So, it may not always be easy to spot rejection.

Rejection also takes many forms. If someone's constantly busy, there's a good chance he's rejecting you. Consider if you were given tickets to the Super Bowl, the Academy Awards, the Olympics, or a flight to the moon, wouldn't you rearrange your schedule to take advantage of these opportunities? Someone who cares about you will rearrange her schedule to spend time with you, even if she's busy. Best not to waste effort on someone who doesn't have time for you.

What if a person suddenly stops responding to your messages or phone calls? Take that as a hint but don't be too hasty. There may be a good reason why the other party hasn't responded. I once went out for coffee with Neil. We had a great time. He said he would call me in a couple of days. I waited and waited and didn't hear from him. After one week, I called him. On his answering machine was this message:

> My father passed away. I've flown back to England
> to attend his funeral and to help out my mother. If
> you need to reach me, call Steve at 650-555-9837.

If I hadn't called him, I wouldn't have realized that the reason he hadn't called had nothing to do with me.

Other Indicators of Lack of Interest

People say and do many things to indicate that they are not interested:

- Not respond to your e-mail, or take more than a couple of weeks to get back to you

- Say "I'll see you around" or "I'll call you soon"—and never do so

- Say "I'll check my schedule and get back to you in a few days"

- Come up with excuses for why they can't get together with you

- Say "I like you as a friend" or "Let's just be friends"

- Not introduce you to their friends

- Appear to be thinking of other matters when you're together

- Never make future plans with you

Some people turn down invitations by telling white lies:

- I'm seeing someone at the moment.

- I have a prior commitment.

- I have a big deadline coming up; I can't afford to take time off right now.

People who don't want to encourage you to ask for an explanation often provide reasons that you can't question:

- I don't feel any chemistry.

- You're a great guy, but I don't see a potential for romance.

- My gut feeling is this isn't going to work.

- You remind me of someone whom I couldn't date (for example, one of my ex's). I realize you're not him, but when I'm with you, I can't get him out of my mind.

If you're not sure whether a person is interested in you, ask. If you're reluctant to do that, rest assured that you aren't alone. Many people would rather not know the answer if it's negative. They don't want to face the end. But isn't it better to know the truth than to waste time with someone who doesn't care to go ahead?

Rejection is an Opportunity

Over twenty-five years ago, Richard Nelson Bolles got laid off. He started looking for a new job, then decided to create one for himself: he helps other people in their search for a career. He's the author of *What Color is Your Parachute? A Practical Manual for Job-Hunters and Career-Changers.* If he hadn't lost his job, he might never have written his perennial best seller.

People who get demoted or fired often end up in a more satisfying job because getting shaken up creates an opportunity to consider what they didn't like about their old jobs and what they prefer.

Remember, winners are rejected more than losers. Authors of best sellers often are rejected first by scores of publishers. John Grisham began his writing career selling *A Time to Kill* out of the trunk of his car. Dating, like book publishing, is a process of failing your way to success.

Rejecting Rejection

How do you overcome fear of rejection? By going out and getting rejected and seeing that it doesn't kill you. Learning to take rejection in stride makes it easier to approach people whom you consider attractive. Reject rejection. Don't let it eat you up; just move on, as many people do when they look for a job. They write to several companies at a time. When they receive a rejection, they improve their cover letter and send it out to more prospective employers. Follow the same strategy in your search for a mate: Check out several people before making any commitment to one. If you get rejected, find more prospects.

For a variety of reasons, not everyone will be interested in you. Some of their reasons will have little to do with who you are. People reject other people for the flimsiest of reasons: your height, the color of your hair, where you attended university, and what you wear. If someone rejects you, don't waste time feeling sorry for yourself. Instead, focus your energy on meeting other people.

After you get rejected, do something that will make you feel good. For example, get a relaxing massage. See a film. Invite a friend out to your favorite restaurant. Take an exciting vacation. Just do something that will put you in a good frame of mind. Overcome your fear of rejection with these tricks:

- Consider the potential benefits of taking advantages of a new opportunity.

- Seek more prospects when your invitation is turned down.

- Increase your self-esteem by doing things that you feel good about. For example, if hiking makes you feel good, go on a hike.

With perseverance and a positive attitude, you'll significantly improve your chances of finding the right person.

Rejecting Other People

Be careful not to say "no" too soon. Realize that first dates are nerve-racking for most of us. Few people shine when they are nervous. Give a person several chances. My mother wasn't impressed with my father on their first date, but she decided to give him a second chance. Now they have been happily married for over forty years.

When to Reject?

When you realize that a person isn't meeting your needs, walk away. A person might not meet your needs by failing to appreciate you, trying to change you, or being overly critical. Move on! Don't spend time with people who treat you poorly or don't think you're great the way you are. Find someone who gives you respect and love.

You can say "no" if you discover someone's abusing some substance, being unfaithful, is emotionally or physically mean, cheats, lies, blames, threatens, intimidates, or does anything that you find unacceptable. Reject the unavailable. Don't waste your time. Look out for *your* best interests.

Consequences of Not Saying "No"

One of the biggest mistakes people make is not realizing when and how to say "no." I was astonished when Laurie told me that she got engaged and married because she didn't feel comfortable breaking up with Joe. I was even more shocked when I heard that two other women got married for the same reason: They didn't want to say "no," even though they had serious reservations.

Don't compromise with the wrong person just because you want a relationship. You'll pay a high price in the long run. When you aren't able to reject, you end up in a relationship, but probably not one you want. Why settle for something that's mediocre? Allow yourself the opportunity to find the love of your life.

Exercise: Why Didn't You Say "No?"

Think of a situation where you didn't say "no" but wish you had. Why didn't you? Mark one or more of the reasons. Feel free to add additional explanations.

☐ I don't want to hurt the other person. I can't be mean.

☐ I'm afraid she won't be my friend afterward.

☐ I'd rather say, "I'm busy." He should know that means, "I'm not interested."

☐ I've gotten into the habit of saying, "I'll call you," and then I purposely don't follow up.

☐ How do I tell him the truth? I don't know how to put it.

☐ I don't have a good reason for saying "no." I feel my reasons are capricious.

☐ I feel I should explain why, but I don't want to sound shallow. His looks just don't turn me on.

☐ I don't want to tell my reasons for rejecting her, because they involve my own prejudices.

☐ I think she just won't listen to what I have to say.

☐ I know he'll try to talk me out of it, so I just don't want to discuss it.

☐ I'm worried that I won't be able to get him to help with my house/car/gardening after I reject him.

☐ I have few enough friends; I don't want to lose one more.

☐ Although our relationship is far from ideal, I'm hesitant to let it go entirely.

☐ I love her. I know I should say "no," but I don't want to close the door completely.

☐ I'm afraid of what he will do. He's been vindictive before.

☐ She has a bad temper.

☐ Other: _____

Review the reasons you checked. Are you interested in learning how to say "no"? Then read on.

How to Reject Other People

When you reject someone, remember that someone else may reject you one day. So think about how you would like to be treated. Ridiculing, teasing, and ignoring are cruel ways to reject an invitation.

If you receive a response to your online personal ad that doesn't interest you, there are several considerate ways to refuse. An easy but cowardly approach is to drop out of existence. Unless there's an earthquake or other natural disaster, not responding to e-mail, like not returning a telephone call, is discourteous. Anyone who was kind enough to express interest in you deserves at least a sensitive "thanks, but no thanks." The person might be thinking about you, even dreaming about you. So don't let his affections linger where he doesn't stand a chance. In the long run, he'll appreciate your letting him know where he stands, even if he doesn't like it. Here are tips for rejecting someone whom you've met:

- Start with a compliment. To boost his self-esteem, tell the person what you appreciated about him and the relationship. For example,

  - I'll have a hard time finding someone as caring and considerate as you are.
  - I love your positive attitude.
  - I've always enjoyed your sense of humor.

  Bad news is usually easier to take if preceded by praise. Then after you've complimented him, lead into what you need to say.

- Be honest about how you feel.

- Make your intentions clear, so that there is no room for ambiguity or misinterpretation. Say "no" with conviction.

- Don't feel obliged to give a reason. If you want to, that's your choice, but it's not necessary and may not help the situation.

- Take responsibility for the relationship not working. Don't blame her. Remember, it's you who are rejecting her. Be willing to be the bad guy.

- Don't change your mind because you feel sorry for the other person. Do what is right for you. The other person may not see it that way, but that's not *your* problem.

- Give him a chance to share his feelings. Empathize with him. "I'm sorry you're finding this painful." But don't try to fix his pain at your own expense. Assure him that you respect his feelings.

- Clearly spell out the terms of the separation so that there is no room for misunderstanding—for example, "Please don't call me. I'll call you when I'm ready."

- If you've just gone out a few times, then rejecting over the telephone or via e-mail is okay.

Here are suggestions for refusing an invitation:

- "Thank you for asking, but I'd rather not."

- "I had a good time last weekend, but I'm not interested in going out again."

- "I enjoy [your sense of humor/your love of life] (be specific), but I am not interested in having a romantic relationship with you."

- Say, "I'll call you" only if you mean it. Even if you do intend to call, don't commit to do so if you might not follow through.

If you say you're involved with someone else, they'll wonder why you're using a dating service. If you say you're busy, they might keep asking and you'll have to keep rejecting. Instead of asking people to interpret "I'm busy" as meaning "I'm not interested," be honest.

A therapist I know advises being honest and using "I" statements like:

- Politics is important to me. I'm looking for someone who shares my interest in making a difference in the world.

- I'm looking for someone who is interested in having children.

- I'm looking for someone who is Jewish.

Be clear in a nice way about what you want. If you aren't attracted to him, better to say it than to lead him on.

Sheila dropped a million hints that she wasn't interested in Fred. But he either chose to ignore them or felt she was playing hard to get. Be direct. Say something like, "I appreciate your interest, but I'm *really* not interested." If he persists, make your point stronger. For example, if he tries to kiss you against your will, you could get his attention by saying, "Isn't this like rape?"

Don't let pressure get to you. Here are suggestions about what you might say if it becomes necessary:

- "There is nothing more to discuss. Bye."

- "Do you understand English? I'm not interested."

- "Please listen to what I am saying. If you don't leave now, I'll call the police."

Chapter 12

Moving to Real Life

In earlier chapters, I talked about how to find and connect with other people over the Internet. In this chapter, I describe how to move your relationship from the Internet to the telephone or a face-to-face meeting.

Moving to the Telephone

You can learn quite a bit about someone's personality, interests, and writing style through e-mail. But there are many things that you can't pick up, such as enthusiasm, energy level, sarcasm, phoniness, and cynicism. Unless you want an Internet-only relationship, consider taking steps to move to talking over the telephone and to meeting in person.

When do you move from the Net to the telephone? When both of you are comfortable doing so. That usually happens some time between an hour after you first connect with each other online to three months later. After my several-month e-mail romance, which I described on page 114, ended as a huge disappointment, I began moving to the telephone after sending two or three e-mail messages.

How do you get a person's telephone number? Typically, a man sends a woman his telephone number. Some send their telephone number in their first e-mail. Other people send it after they have exchanged several messages. Most wait until after the subject of telephone numbers comes up in conversation. Sometimes, one person requests the other person's number.

Rosanne sent Josh a message letting him know she found his profile intriguing. Josh checked out hers and was pleased with what he found. He quickly sent back a short note saying, "You sound like an interesting person. I also love the city. I go there several times a week. Call me if you'd like to know more. My telephone number is 415-555-2643."

Josh realized that, if Rosanne was interested, she could call him and still remain anonymous; she wouldn't have to reveal her real name or telephone number. He figured he was making it easier on a woman and it was also easier for him, since he didn't have to ask for her telephone number.

Rosanne didn't call back the day she received Josh's e-mail. The following day Josh sent another e-mail with his telephone number, just in case Rosanne lost or misplaced his first message.

If you make a call, don't necessarily expect to remain anonymous. People who subscribe to CallerID obtain your telephone number, and sometimes your name, if you haven't blocked CallerID on your line—even if they don't answer the telephone! If you wish to remain anonymous, block CallerID before placing a call. In many locations you can do this by pressing *67 (1167 on rotary telephones) before dialing, but consult your telephone book or telephone company for instructions that apply to you. Or call from a pay phone, or have CallerID permanently blocked.

Not everyone exchanges telephone numbers as quickly as Josh and Rosanne. Many people send four or five lengthy e-mail messages before moving to the telephone. Here's why some people are apprehensive about giving out their telephone numbers:

- If someone were to call and say, "Hello, this is Paul," she might not be sure which Paul is on the line.

- She wants to review the other person's profile and e-mail directly before speaking with him. She can do so, if she makes the call.

- He is hardly ever reachable by telephone. He may travel a great deal. So if someone were to call him, chances are she wouldn't reach him.

- She is living with other people—perhaps roommates, an ex-lover, a parent, or children, and would rather keep her personal matters private.

- She strives to minimize her chances of getting into dangerous or uncomfortable situations. She would rather not leave herself vulnerable to telephone harassment. She gives out little personal information to minimize the chances of unwanted strangers tracking her down.

- He's married or involved in a relationship and is not completely honest with his partner. Florence asked one married guy how his wife would feel if she learned of his interest in getting together with her. Instead of answering her question, he said he wouldn't mind if his wife had an affair. "No, that wasn't what I asked. How would *she* feel?" wrote Florence. She never heard back from him.

It's usually best to be sensitive to someone's reluctance to give out his number. Pressure often has an effect opposite to that intended.

You probably aren't a serial killer, and perhaps you find it insulting that someone would consider treating you as a threat. But think about it from the other person's perspective. Say you were a serial killer, what should the other person do? Wouldn't it be prudent for her not to give you her number? It's better to play it safe than to be sorry. Hopefully, with time, she'll realize that it's to her advantage to give you her number.

Be Careful What You Say

Martin had a bad experience with a woman who filled up his answering machine with messages, so he was reluctant to give out his telephone number again. Florence decided to do her own sleuthing to see whether she could figure out his number. When Martin called her, he mentioned that he was selling his Harley Davidson motorcycle and his BMW. Florence guessed that he would advertise them in the local newspaper. So she got online and scanned through the classified ads for Harley Davidson motorcycles and BMWs looking to see if any of them listed the same telephone number. One did. She called the number and to her delight she heard Martin's voice on the answering machine. She didn't leave a message but instead sent him an e-mail message with his telephone number, just to show him that, even though he wasn't willing to give it out, she was able to figure it out. Martin was annoyed. Morals of this story are:

- *If you don't want someone to know what your telephone number is or who you are, don't give out information that could lead them to you.*

- *Don't track down someone's telephone number if he makes it clear he doesn't want you to have it.*

What to Talk About

How do you start a conversation? Introduce yourself: "Hello, this is Nancy from Hearts Online (*name of the matchmaking service you used*), but you also know me as `Fervent`." Use the telephone to check out someone's character: Is his telephone personality consistent with his e-mail one? Consider discussing questions mentioned in Chapter 10. Or use the telephone to arrange the logistics of meeting, and save your questions for when you meet.

Encouraging Someone to Ask You Out

This section contains advice for women who want to be asked out by a man, but it is also applicable to men who want to be asked out by women. A man is more willing to ask out a woman whom he feels is likely to accept his invitation. So if you want to be asked out, let him know. Write, for instance,

> I'd like to get to know you better. I'm
> interested in meeting you.

Perhaps you think that you don't need to be so explicit. But people are not necessarily able to guess your meaning if you send "signals." Make your interests clear. You are in essence asking a man out, but you're giving him the chance to feel as though he is initiating, and our society has trained him to take that role.

I used to ask men out, but I find that this technique is more effective. If a man doesn't want to go out with me, I don't want to go out with him. Many men have little experience turning down invitations. Some just postpone and postpone, instead of rejecting. Other people go out, but their hearts aren't in it. I would rather make my interest clear and spend my time with men who choose to take the initiative and ask me out.

Meeting Face to Face

If you're getting along via e-mail and on the telephone, why not take the opportunity to see whether you also get along in person? By meeting face to face, you'll get to see how he carries himself, what he looks like, how he interacts with other people, and whether you feel any chemistry.

Some people move directly from the Net to a face-to-face meeting—they don't bother with the telephone. That's what Eve and Jeremy did. They corresponded by e-mail for three weeks. Jeremy gave Eve his telephone number, but she didn't call. Instead of asking for her number, Jeremy suggested meeting in a café. On the fateful day, Eve couldn't find the designated place. Jeremy waited at the café for nearly an hour. He couldn't call her because he didn't have her number. Jeremy thought Eve was standing him up.

Eve drove home to retrieve Jeremy's telephone number from her computer. She called his office. Fortunately, his pager number was on his answering machine. So she paged Jeremy; he called her back and gave her directions to the café. She drove there, and they finally met.

More commonly, people first talk on the telephone; then, if they hit it off, they meet face to face. Not Mark and Florence. Although their first telephone conversation went swimmingly, they were apprehensive about meeting face to face because they both felt uncomfortable about being overweight. So they talked on the telephone for about two weeks before arranging their first meeting.

Nathan moves his cyber relationships along by expressing interest in meeting a woman face to face so that he can get to know her in person. Most women respond favorably.

Sam and Claire arranged to meet for lunch. Claire told Sam what she would be wearing. When she arrived she saw a man who fit Sam's description eyeing people from across the street. He never crossed the street. Claire suspected that Sam didn't like her looks, and so had stood her up. At first Claire was upset. But she got over it after deciding that she wouldn't want to go out with someone who would do such a thing.

Why wouldn't a person want to meet face to face?

- She's contacted other men who sound much more interesting, and is checking them out first.

- He's extremely busy at the moment and doesn't want to take the time to get together yet.

- She lives far away and it's both expensive and time consuming to meet.

- He lied about himself and would rather that you not find out quite yet.

Don't get down on yourself if your face-to-face meetings go poorly. Blind dates are nerve-racking experiences for most people. Go on at least a dozen blind dates before you decide that the experience isn't for you.

If you're interested in going out again after meeting someone, get in touch with the person. Share what you enjoyed about your date. Most people appreciate a "thank you" or a few kind words.

What to Do and What to Avoid

When you do decide to meet, take precautions:

- Tell a friend where you're going and for how long you'll be gone. Give the name and telephone number of the person you're meeting. Call your friend when the date is over.
- Take your own car or transportation. Bring enough money to get home on your own.
- Don't give out your home address.
- Meet in a public, well lit, well populated place.
- Do not go to her home or invite her to yours.
- If you're traveling far from home, stay in a hotel, in a bed and breakfast, or with a friend. Arrange your own transportation.

Here are suggestions for your first meeting:

- Pick activities that you both like. Both of you should have a say in the decision making.

- Spend an appropriate amount of money. You don't have to break the bank. Excessive spending or frugality will make your date uncomfortable. When your date is paying at a restaurant, you can't lose when you order something in the middle price range.

- Women: Offer to split the check.

- Have lunch, coffee, or brunch (rather than dinner). These days, many people meet for coffee. Don't make a big time commitment before you meet. There's no sense in spending lots of time with someone who may not be right for you.

- Work on creating a good first impression. Arrive on time. Stand up straight. Wear clothes that make you feel good about yourself. Treat your date with respect.

- Limit consumption of alcohol. After you drink, you may feel more relaxed, but you may behave in an unattractive manner.

Be honest about your feelings. Don't expect a date to be able to read your mind. After I changed our first meeting from dinner to coffee after dinner, Ralph e-mailed me the following note:

> I was a bit miffed when you changed the
> plan. My initial reaction was that you
> got a better offer and don't really know
> me so that's what happens. Oh well, kind
> of typical of "blind dates" and that's
> what happens in the dating world.

Here's how I responded:

> The reason that I postponed our meeting
> was so that I could have dinner with my
> parents and old family friends who live
> in LA. This was the first time they visited

> since my parents moved to their retirement
> home. I want to make sure to spend time
> with them while I have the opportunity.
> Just thinking about them getting older
> and dying is bringing tears to my eyes
> right now. I'm sorry you felt miffed by
> my change of plans.

After we got together, Ralph wrote back:

> Thanks for the explanation about the change
> of plans. I certainly understand from
> a variety of perspectives and feel much
> more comfortable now that you have shared
> with me what was going on for you.

When you change plans, consider explaining why you are doing so, particularly if you have a good reason.

Telling How You Met

Some people worry about what they will say when friends and relatives ask how they met. Suppose that your first meeting in the physical world is at a bookstore; you could tell your friends that you met through the Internet, or that you first met in a bookstore. Both are true.

I first met David at a reception at the Business School Entrepreneur's Forum. Then one week after we met, he invited me to a party at his house. Since I figured people at the party might ask me how we met, I asked what he would prefer I tell them. Should I say, "We met each other at the reception at the Business School Entrepreneur's Forum"? But what if people then ask David where he got the idea to attend that event, and whether he thought he would meet a woman there?

We decided that we would tell people that we met through an online matchmaking service. We thought that it would be best for David's friends to learn that people do meet decent people through the Internet. If we were open about our experience, perhaps other people would be also. We might find out that other couples met through the Internet. Finally, it's a good way to let friends know that you are serious about looking for a relationship.

Success Stories

Let me share a few success stories with you.

Lisa and Patrick

Before putting her profile online, Lisa put together a list of qualities that she considered important in a man. She believed the list would help her to evaluate men who contacted her.

Immediately after she posted her profile, Lisa received a huge amount of e-mail. Although she had access to the Internet at work, she picked up her e-mail from home. She tried to keep up a correspondence with over forty men. She kept a spreadsheet on all the men so that she wouldn't get them confused (see page 192).

She found the quality of the men to be high and that they often matched her preferred characteristics. She enjoyed corresponding with them via e-mail, and eventually met fourteen of them for lunch or coffee; some of them she met several times, and a few became good friends. All that happened in less than six weeks!

Her dream man, Patrick, contacted her the day after Valentine's Day; they met a week later after exchanging numerous intense e-mail messages. She felt she knew him before she met him in person. When they met, they were attracted to each other. He had most of the qualities that she was seeking—the only ones he didn't have involved his body: he was overweight, but she decided that she didn't mind. She knew right away that Patrick was the one for her, that she didn't need to keep looking for another man. Soon after, she made her profile not visible to other users (she was exhausted anyway!).

Patrick was better than Lisa could have imagined. He was eager to get involved with her kids, built a great tree house for her 7-year-old son, and wanted to repair things in her house—and he knew what he was doing, unlike most men she had encountered. He was funny, smart, kind, and sensitive. Being in a relationship was his number one priority.

They have been together on a daily basis for nearly one year, and it seems more and more that this might be a lifelong relationship.

She thanks the online matchmaking service for helping her to find happiness with the right man. She found the service to be affordable, easy to use, fun, and safe. (She had no problems with any of the men.) If her relationship with Patrick doesn't work out, she'll definitely post another ad online.

Eve and Jeremy

Eve's good friend Adam suggested that she try using an online matchmaking service. Eve and Adam wrote her ad together. The headline was "Artistic Chick Seeks Bright Stable Man." Adam put the ad online since Eve didn't have Internet access. For the first two weeks, Adam printed out Eve's responses and gave them to her. After a couple of weeks, she bought her own modem and got online.

Lots of guys wrote to Eve, but she was still angry at men for past betrayals, so she wrote back sarcastic hostile notes. Many were put off by her negative tone.

Jeremy, an old time Internet user, was enamored with the technology and would cruise the Web regularly looking for new interesting sites. He found an online matchmaking site and, shortly thereafter, Eve's ad.

Jeremy was not put off by Eve's hostile tone. He just humored her. After three weeks of writing to her several times a day,

Jeremy invited Eve for coffee.

Although they had not exchanged photographs, when she walked in the café, Jeremy knew who she was. They hit it off right from the start. Before he departed, Jeremy invited Eve to go for a hike that Saturday. After their hike, he asked her out again. This pattern—Jeremy asking Eve out at the end of their get together—continued for many more dates. They grew closer and closer. Eighteen months later, they got married. Now they are living happily together in San Francisco.

Mary and Tom

Mary placed the following ad:

> *Handle:* triplescorpio
> *Headline:* A Transformational Experience
>
> I'm childless, living in Palo Alto for
> the last 23 years, blessed with many friends.
> I'm about as deep as they come. Wonderfully
> loving, sexy, adventurous, growthful, spiritual.
> A combination of the highly practical (working
> in the computer industry for over 15 years),
> and the highly transformational (developing
> a practice as a psychotherapist). I have
> been a professor, a computer industry manager
> and product creator. I'm currently developing
> a psychotherapy practice working with an
> emphasis on couples and on people who have
> life-threatening illnesses--in particular,
> women who are struggling with breast cancer
> (and their partners and families). I'm
> a private pilot (though not current), and
> I love golf, skiing, dancing, films, reading,
> walking and hiking. I am a member of Unity

> Church of Palo Alto. I want a Pisces,
> Cancer, Scorpio, or Taurus male born in
> 1938, 1939, 1942, 1944, 1947, 1950, 1951,
> or 1954. I want someone who is well-educated
> and also spiritual, who sees relationship
> as a royal road to personal growth, and
> who is excited about life and loving.

It sounds like Mary is shopping for a man much as other people might shop for bottles of wine: by the year! For Mary, a man's birth month and year is important. Tom wasn't born in any of the years listed in the ad, but he considers himself spiritual and shares Mary's interests in golf, flying, dancing, and computers. So he wrote to her. In her reply, Mary acknowledged that they did seem to share many interests, but she wasn't interested in meeting him because of the year in which he was born.

Tom wrote back, "You mean you're going to dismiss me entirely because of the year I was born?"

"That's right. Good luck in searching for the 'right one.' "

Tom challenged her, but in a respectful way that perked her interest. "Am I correct that you are not interested in talking on the telephone because of the year I was born?"

After Mary confirmed that was true, Tom wrote, "Thanks for admitting it."

Tom was the only man who questioned her rejection. Mary decided to give him a chance and met him for dinner.

When he entered in the restaurant, Mary knew Tom wasn't the one for her. He didn't fit her image: he was not tall enough. She didn't fit his image: she was too old.

They also didn't hit it off in conversation. At the end of the meal, Tom suggested taking a walk. Mary was a bit taken aback, since it was obvious to her that there was no chemistry. Tom figured that if they talked a bit longer, maybe they would find some sort of connection.

It was during the walk, that Mary mentioned her interest in tantra yoga. Suddenly, Tom's ears perked up since he has been looking for someone with whom to attend a tantra yoga workshop. From that moment on, things just seemed to click. Tom became more interested and animated.

Several days later, they went out for a second date, during which time they shared personal information with each other. At first, they were both dating other people. But after about two months, Mary asked Tom if he would be willing to date her exclusively. He said no, so they split up. Three weeks without Mary convinced Tom that he would rather have her back in his life. So he stopped dating other women, took his ad offline, and got back together with Mary. A week after that, Mary was diagnosed as having breast cancer; I mentioned her story on page 129. Being with each other through Mary's mastectomy and Tom's heart attack has strengthened their relationship. Despite Tom not being born in one of the years that Mary specified, they have a solid relationship.

Going Online

The Internet can provide a safe, inexpensive, and time-efficient way to find someone to love. It's often difficult to take the first step, but I encourage you to do it. Dating gives you opportunities to visit new places, to meet new people, to learn about yourself, and to experience love. Take a chance. Create more opportunities. *Put your heart online!*

Appendices

Myth: It's only a matter of time before you'll meet some-one.

If you haven't made the right connection, enlarge your social circle.

Appendix A

Technical Information

This Appendix provides a brief introduction to the Internet, the World Wide Web, and encryption. It also discusses how to include a photograph in an e-mail message.

Understanding the Web

The *World Wide Web*, also known as the *Web*, is a collection of information stored on various computers around the world. To get on the Web, you must have access to the Internet and a Web browser. Netscape Navigator, Internet Explorer, and Mosaic are examples of Web browsers. You can download some browsers from the Internet for free. Browsers are also available for sale in computer stores.

Getting on the Internet

One common approach to getting on the Internet is asking someone who is on it to help you. Many people ask a friend. If you find someone attractive to assist you and things go well, who knows, you might not need the Internet, at least not for finding a date.

Here are the basics about getting on the Internet, in case you do it yourself. You need access to a computer with a modem and telephone line. Many people use personal computers running the Microsoft Windows or the Macintosh operating system. It's best to use a computer with *at least* 8 megabytes (MB) of RAM; with more RAM you will get significantly better performance.

You don't need to own a computer, you just need to be able to log into one. So you could use a friend's, one at work or at a library, or you could rent time on a computer. If you don't have a direct connection, you need a telephone line, but you don't need a separate telephone line for the computer nor a separate jack. A telephone that's plugged into the wall can instead be plugged into the modem, while the modem, in turn, is plugged into the telephone jack. Thus one line can be shared by your computer and your telephone, although you can't use both at the same time.

If you are using a modem, you need access to the Internet through an Internet Service Provider (ISP) or a commercial on-line service (COS). ISPs do what their name implies: they provide service or access to the Internet. Most ISPs provide software for dialing up to their service and connecting to the Internet, and help getting started. Some ISPs offer browsers. Ask your local computer store or computer user group for ISPs in your area. See `thelist.internet.com` or `www.internet.com` for a list of ISPs.

Commercial online services, such as America Online (AOL), CompuServe, and Prodigy, also offer online access and telephone support. They typically provide discussion groups (sometimes known as forums), chat rooms, e-mail, online events, and Internet access. Here are some telephone numbers:

Service	Telephone Numbers
America Online (AOL)	800-827-6364; 703-448-8700
CompuServe	800-848-8990; 614-718-2800
Prodigy	800-776-3449; 914-448-8000
Microsoft Network (MSN)	800-386-5550
Delphi	800-695-4005; 617-441-4801

An ISP or COS typically provides software for dialing up to its service. Install software and then follow the directions for connecting to the Internet.

Here are some good books for learning more about the Internet and how to use it:

- Krol, Ed and Bruce C. Klopfenstein. *The Whole Internet User's Guide & Catalog*, (O'Reilly, 1996)

- Krol, Ed and Paula Ferguson. *The Whole Internet for Windows 95 Users Guide & Catalog* (O'Reilly, 1995)

- Levine, John, Margaret Levine Young, and Arnold Reinhold. *Internet for Dummies Quick Reference* (IDG Books World Wide, 1997)

- Levine, John, Margaret Levine Young, and Arnold Reinhold. *Internet for Dummies* (IDG Books World Wide, 1997)

Getting on the Web

After installing your browser, access a Web page by connecting to the Internet, starting your browser, and entering in the location field the Web address, also known as URL (Universal Resource Locator), for the page you would like to see. URLs consist of three parts:

1. Document access type, followed by a colon and two slashes (`://`). Access types include:

> http For hypertext, i.e., Web pages (default).
> ftp For transferring files via *F*ile *T*ransfer *P*rotocol.
> mailto For sending e-mail.

2. Host name of the computer being accessed, followed by a slash (/), which can be omitted if it is the last character of the URL.

3. The path to the file that contains the information.

Consider

> http://www.HeartsOnline.com/services.html

The http indicates we are accessing a hypertext document or Web page. The Web page services.html is stored on the computer named www.HeartsOnline.com.

The home page is the top level document for an individual or an institution. The Hearts Online home page can be found at http://www.HeartsOnline.com.

Finding Hearts Online's Web Site

Visit my Hearts Online Web site to learn about online matchmaking services, by entering the address www.HeartsOnline.com in your browser. When you are connected, click on highlighted text—a link—and your browser gathers more information (which may be stored halfway around the world and on various Web pages) and displays it. Click on a link for an online matchmaking service, such as Matchmaker, and their homepage appears in your browser.

Most browsers give you the option of adding a site to a list of places you want to re-visit. I recommend bookmarking the Hearts Online homepage, URL http://www.HeartsOnline.com. After visiting this page, just perform one of the following procedures:

Netscape Navigator calls these bookmarks. To add Hearts Online as a bookmark, go to the page and click on the **Bookmarks** menu item or icon, then select the option to **Add Bookmark**. Once you've done that, to use the bookmark, select the bookmark directly from the **Bookmarks** menu.

Lynx also calls them bookmarks. To add Hearts Online as a bookmark, go to the page and type 'a' (for **add bookmark**) and then type 'd' (saving the **document** to a bookmark file). To use the bookmark, simply type 'v' (for **view bookmarks**) and, using the up/down arrow or tab keys if necessary, move to Hearts Online then hit `return` or `enter`.

NCSA Mosaic calls bookmarks your *Hot List*. To add Hearts Online to your Hot List, go to the page and click on the menu item **Navigate**, then select the option **Add This Document**. To use the Hot List entry to get to Hearts Online, go under the top menu item **Navigate**, and select the the option **Hotlist**.... Then double-click on **Hearts Online**.

Microsoft Internet Explorer calls this same feature your *Favorites*. To add Hearts Online, go to the home page and click on **Favorites**, then select the option **Add Page to Favorites**. You can then get to Hearts Online by selecting it from the **Favorites menu**.

Dealing with Photographs

How can you make your picture available to those you meet? First you need a scanned image. Here are several ways to do this:

- Get a camera that produces digital images.

- Bring your film to a lab that can produce digital images of your negatives.

- Send your photograph to a matchmaking service. Many will scan your photograph for free and put it on their site.

- Bring a photograph to a desktop publishing or photocopying service and have them produce scanned images of your photographs.

- Purchase a scanner and scan your own photographs.

Attaching your Image

Many e-mail programs allow you to attach a photograph to an e-mail message. Typically you do this by starting up your mail program, then hitting a button labeled `Attach`. You will be asked to specify the name and location of the file to be attached. Many e-mail programs support a variety of image types include `jpg` (also known as jpeg) and `gif`.

Using Encryption

When you send an e-mail message to someone, it may pass through many computers to reach its destination. Someone can intercept it and read it before it is sent, while it is traveling, or after it has reached its destination. When you send personal e-mail messages, one of your co-worker or someone who doesn't even know you, can find out about your private life. You can make your e-mail difficult to read by encrypting it. These days, few people do so, though some e-mail programs provide encryption capabilities. How important your privacy is to you? If it's important, encrypt your messages.

PGP

PGP or *Pretty* *Good* *Privacy* is a freeware encryption program. PGP is free for noncommercial use. There are also commercial versions, which are easier to use. For more on PGP, check the following Web pages:

```
http://www.pgp.com
http://web.mit.edu/network/pgp/html (US & Canada)
http://www.ifi.uio.no/pgp (other parts of the world)
```

Appendix B

Other Places on the Net

To find dates in the real world, go on a bicycle trip or a safari, volunteer for a charity, take dance lessons or a cooking class, get involved in a political campaign, or join a church or religious organization. Get out and become involved. Just as you would in the real world, it's best to find people online who share your passions. This Appendix describes how to learn about events and activities through discussion groups, chat rooms, and the World Wide Web.

World Wide Web

The World Wide Web is a great information resource about companies, clubs, and other organizations, as well as places, people, events, and activities. I've used the Web to read film reviews, get train schedules, find local clubs, and sign up for conferences, learn about particular people, and see their photographs and articles. I find the sheer quantity of information on the Web truly astounding. When looking up a particular topic, I have often discovered other interesting Web pages by following links from one page to another.

Consider putting up your own Web page. Use it to tell other people about yourself and show what you look like. When someone wants to know more about you, point him to your Web page by giving him the URL.

Directories and Search Engines

Web directories and search engines are designed to assist you in finding more information about particular topics. A Web directory provides hierarchical catalogs of the Web. Directories are like the subject card catalogs that used to be in the library before they were computerized. The contents are broken down to topics and subtopics. Here are headings on Yahoo (`www.yahoo.com`):

Arts and Humanities	Architecture, Photography, Literature...
Business and Economy	Companies, Finance, Employment...
Computers and Internet	Internet, WWW, Software, Multimedia...
Education	Universities, K-12, College Entrance...
Entertainment	Cool Links, Movies, Music, Humor...
Government	Military, Politics, Law, Taxes...
Health	Medicine, Drugs, Diseases, Fitness...
News and Media	Current Events, Magazines, TV...
Recreation and Sports	Sports, Games, Travel, Autos, Outdoors...
Reference	Libraries, Dictionaries, Phone Numbers...
Regional	Countries, Regions, U.S. States...
Science	CS, Biology, Astronomy, Engineering...
Social Science	Anthropology, Sociology, Economics...
Society and Culture	People, Environment, Religion...

When you click on a category or subcategory, you'll be taken to another page with further refined categories and URLs for Web pages relating to your selection.

Here are URLs for some popular Web directories:

Excite!	`www.excite.com`
Infoseek	`www.infoseek.com`
Lycos	`www.lycos.com`
Yahoo!	`www.yahoo.com`

There are Web scouts that traverse the World Wide Web creating indexes. These scouts start by visiting familiar Web pages and follow links on those pages to new pages. The scouts then make this information available through *search engines*. Here is a list of some popular search engines:

AltaVista	`www.altavista.digital.com`
Dogpile	`www.dogpile.com`
Excite!	`www.excite.com`
Hotbot	`www.hotbot.com`
Infoseek	`www.infoseek.com`
Lycos	`www.lycos.com`
Metacrawler	`www.metacrawler.com`
Webcrawler	`www.webcrawler.com`
Yahoo!	`www.yahoo.com`

Type in a word or phrase of something that interests you, e.g., "roller blade" (quotes and all), then instruct the search engine to start looking. Typically within seconds, the search engine will present you with at least several and sometimes as many as hundreds or thousands of documents that reference the word or phrase you requested. Different search engines work differently. Test drive several to determine the ones you prefer to use.

Recently, I decided that I would like to rent a tandem—a bicycle built for two. I asked several local bicycle stores if they have them. Unfortunately, I didn't find any that did. So I turned to the Web. Using the Alta Vista search engine, I looked up "tandem bicycle" and found the Bay Area Roaming Tandems, a San Francisco Bay Area club. I sent an e-mail to a club member informing her of my interest. She sent me a complimentary copy of their newsletter, which had ads from stores that rent and sell tandems.

Surfing the Web

Since the Web contains an enormous amount of information, both relevant and irrelevant, it is sometimes difficult to find information that interests you. Here are some suggestions:

- Look up the Web pages of people you know or have heard of. Follow links on their Web pages.
- Find Web pages for organizations that interest you.
- Look for items you want to buy, e.g., tickets to events, clothes, cars, houses, etc.
- Visit prospective date's sites, particularly before a rendezvous. Some people have personal Web pages. Other people are mentioned in their employer's Web page. People who have companies sometimes have a corporate Web page.

E-Mail Address Lookup

If you know someone's name, how can you find his e-mail address given that he has one? Here are a few suggestions:

- Keep an e-mail address book. When someone sends you e-mail, copy his name and return address into your electronic address book.
- If you have someone's business card, check whether it has his e-mail address.
- Check various white pages directory services, which are online and similar to the white pages of your city's telephone book.

  Four11 (`www.four11.com`) — With this online user directory you can look up a person's e-mail address and home page. It also has telephone numbers, yellow pages, travel deals, and housing listings for renters, buyers, and sellers.

Switchboard (www.switchboard.com) — With Switchboard you can find people, businesses, Web sites, and e-mail addresses.

WhoWhere (www.whowhere.com) — According to their home page, WhoWhere is "the way to find people on the Web." You can look up e-mail addresses, telephone and post addresses, yellow pages, home pages, government agencies, and even ancestors. WhoWhere is linked to other services where you can buy and sell cars and houses, among other things.

- Use a search engine to look up a person's name. Check whether any of the Web pages found by the search engine provides an e-mail address.

Directions Lookup

If you plan to meet someone at a physical, as opposed to cyber, location, you can often obtain detailed directions and a map using an online map service. Here are a few services that offer online maps and directions:

Lucent's Maps On Us	www.mapsonus.com
MapQuest	www.mapquest.com
Vicinity Corp.'s MapBlast	www.mapblast.com
Xerox PARC Map Server	pubweb.parc.xerox.com/map

Ted impressed some of his dates by finding his way to cafés and restaurants given only their street address. Ted's secret weapon is MapQuest.

Discussion Groups

The Internet connects people all over the world. When the Internet was initially established, people used it to send e-mail messages to each other. As with physical mail, e-mail must have the address of the recipient. In 1979-80, Steve Bellovin, Jim Ellis, Tom Truscott, and Steve Daniel at Duke University implemented a distributed bulletin board system supported mainly by UNIX machines. It became known as Usenet, which was short for "Users' Network," and because it was free and non-proprietary, it swiftly became international in scope. It's now one of the largest information resources in existence.

There are other services that support online discussion. Other popular services include The Well (`www.well.com`) and Echo, which stands for East Coast Hang out.

Millions of people from all over the world talk about anything and everything. Users submit postings to discussion groups, known as newsgroups on Usenet and forums on the Well. There are several thousand newsgroups covering topics like atheism, investing, job opportunities, music, tennis, and feminism. There are even newsgroups on David Letterman, Madonna, and Jimmy Buffett. Here are the names of just a few:

```
alt.aldus.pagemaker       biz.books.technical
alt.atheism.moderated     misc.invest.real-estate
alt.fan.letterman         misc.jobs.offered
alt.fan.madonna           rec.aviation.soaring
alt.fan.jimmy-buffett     rec.food.recipes
alt.personals             rec.music.classical.guitar
alt.personals.ads         rec.sport.tennis
ba.personals              soc.feminism
```

Discussion groups can be *unmoderated* (anyone can post) or *moderated* (submissions are automatically directed to a moderator, who edits or filters them). Some discussion groups have parallel mailing lists, with postings to a group automatically propagated to its mailing list and vice versa. Some moderated groups are even distributed as *digests*, with groups of postings periodically collected into a single large posting with an index.

Discussion groups can get a huge volume of traffic and they can be a great source of information. Some people post questions; other people post helpful information; still other people post so that they can see their name in print. Unfortunately, in the last few years, discussion groups have been flooded with *spam*,[1] irrelevant, inappropriate, or unsolicited and unwanted material, e.g., get-rich-quick schemes, pointers to sex sites, and chain letters. You might have to wade through lots of material before finding articles that interest you. Spam is generally filtered out of moderated groups and digests.

Consider subscribing to newsgroups, forums, lists, and digests on topics you find interesting. They bring together people with common interests, providing you an opportunity to participate in discussions. Read messages and send e-mail to the authors of interesting articles. Post messages so that other people can learn of your existence. I know several people who met their partners through discussion groups. They had the opportunity to learn about each other in a non-threatening situation—in the comfort of their own homes, as opposed to on a nerve-racking first date.

Newsgroup Names

Newsgroups are gathered into several large areas or trees, each of which is broken into subareas or sub-trees. The different parts are always separated by "." (period). The first part of a newsgroup name is called its *hierarchy*. Consider, for instance, the name `rec.sport.tennis`. This newsgroup is in the `rec` or recreational area, in the `sports` subtree. Within each newsgroup, there are messages (also referred to as *articles* or *postings*) that

---

[1]The word *spam* comes from the Monty Python *Spam* song.

look like e-mail between one user and another. But instead of just being sent between two people, these messages are available to anyone with access to Usenet. The most popular Usenet newsgroup hierarchies are:

comp	Relating to computers.
sci	Relating to the sciences.
rec	Relating to recreation, e.g., sports, hobbies, arts.
soc	Relating to social interests.
news	Relating to netnews itself.
misc	Miscellaneous topics.
talk	Long arguments, frequently political.
alt	For alternative discussions.

Regional, organizational, and national hierarchies also exist. They include:

ba	San Francisco Bay Area
ny	New York
uk	United Kingdom
ibm	IBM

There are hierarchies serving languages other than English, such as:

de	German (Deutsch)
es	Spanish (Español)
fj	Japanese
fr	French

Cooking up a Meeting

Monica has always liked cooking. She's an active participant in rec.food.recipes. One day Paul e-mailed her a note complimenting one of the recipes she posted to the Net, and they started corresponding. Paul lives near Eureka in Northern California, about 300 miles from Monica, who lives in the San Francisco Bay Area, so it wasn't easy for them to meet.

Many people in the San Francisco Bay Area who subscribe to `rec.food.recipes` periodically have dinner parties where they can sample food and socialize. Wanting to meet Monica, Paul decided to drive down for one of these parties. They instantly hit it off. Now every couple of weeks, either he drives down to visit Monica or she drives up to visit Paul.

Reading Usenet News (a.k.a. netnews)

How you read netnews depends on what computer and software you use. Online services, such as America Online (AOL), CompuServe, and Prodigy, and Internet Service Providers (ISPs) should be able to provide instructions on how to read netnews using their system. You can also perhaps get pointers from other users on your system.

Posting an Article

To familiarize yourself with a newsgroup, read *at least* a dozen articles in it before posting anything. In many newsgroups, periodically an expert posts a list of Frequently Asked Questions (FAQ) together with answers. Read a newsgroup's FAQ to check whether someone else has posted the same question or comment or posted the information you're posting or would like to obtain.

If your article is intended for one person or several people, don't post it to the newsgroup. Instead, send e-mail directly to those people.

♡♡♡

Usenet is in the public domain. Be aware that anyone can read what you post, even those that don't currently have access to the Internet, for Usenet articles are archived and indexed. Years from now, someone can look up what you said back in 1998. So think carefully before you post things like your home address, telephone number, opinions, or rude remarks.

♡♡♡

Because of the huge amount of data posted to Usenet daily, almost all articles expire after a few days. Expired articles are deleted and are not viewable by users any more, except through Deja News and other archives.

Deja News (`www.dejanews.com`)

Deja News offers a Web interface to Internet Discussion Groups, providing a way to search, read, and participate in discussions. Deja News doesn't expire articles; they archive Usenet news, mailing lists, and digests and plan to keep them forever. Here is a summary of the capabilities Deja News offers:

- *Keyword Searching* — Search for specific keywords, e.g., use keyword searching to find places to hike in Northern California.

- *Search Filtering* — Search for articles by dates, authors, and subjects, e.g., look up articles written by someone who posts infrequently to `misc.invest`.

- *Interest Finder* — Search for discussion groups where your keywords appear most often. This capability is a great way to identify groups you're likely to find of interest.

- *Message Posting* — Get involved in thousands of ongoing discussions. Share your thoughts, opinions, or expertise with people around the world!

- *Reading* — The *Read News* interface allows you to read current messages.

Mailing Lists

People with shared interests can send messages to each other and hold group discussions via mailing lists. Mailing lists differ from newsgroups in that a separate copy of each message is e-mailed to each member of the list. Mailing lists are generally smaller, more focused, more intimate, and less active than newsgroups.

Each mailing list has its own e-mail addresses. Most lists just forward e-mail sent to the list. Other lists are filtered by humans or programs; lists edited or filtered by humans are called *moderated*. People on the list respond to messages and thus contribute to the discussion. Every mailing list has at least two addresses:

The list address. E-mail messages sent to this address are forwarded to subscribers of the list.

The administrative address. Messages sent to the administrative address are read only by the list's coordinator(s). Send messages to this address to subscribe and unsubscribe. Often messages sent to the administrative address are processed entirely by a computer program, called a *mail server* or *list server*, a.k.a. listserv. In this case, your message needs to be written in a specific format for the list server to process it. Often the list server will automatically send a response to all requests it receives.

Finding a Mailing List

Find the address of a mailing list from someone who is on the list or from an index of mailing lists. Here are addresses for two Web sites that maintain indexes:

http://www.liszt.com — You can search the main directory or browse topics, such as:

Business	Finance, Jobs, Marketing ...
Computers	Internet, Database, Programming ...
Culture	Gay, Jewish, Parenting ...
Education	Distance Education, Academia, Internet ...
Health	Medicine, Allergy, Support ...
Humanities	Philosophy, History, Psychology ...
Music	Bands, Singer-Songwriters, Genres ...
Nature	Animals, Environment, Plants ...
News	International, Regional, Politics ...
Politics	Environment, Activism, Human Rights ...
Recreation	Games, Autos, Sports ...
Religion	Christian, Jewish, Women ...
Science	Biology, Astronomy, Chemistry ...
Social	Regional, Religion, Kids ...

http://www.neosoft.com/internet/paml — The acronym paml stands for Publicly Accessible Mailing Lists. You can use paml's search engine to look for mailings on a particular topic. If you know the name of the list or are looking for lists on a general topic, try their index page. They maintain two indexes: a simple alphabetical index and a subject index.

Getting On and Off a Mailing List

The way you get on (subscribe to) or off (unsubscribe from) a mailing list depends on how the list is maintained. For lists maintained by a person, send an e-mail message to the list maintainer asking to be added or removed from their list, e.g., "Please add me to your party mailing list" or "Please remove me from your investment club mailing list." Be polite and include the address where you would like the mailing list messages to be sent.

For lists maintained by a computer, you need to write in a fixed format. To join a list that is maintained by a computer program, often you send e-mail to the administrative address with the body of your message containing:

SUBSCRIBE *listname YourFirstName YourLastName*

For example, to subscribe to the CINEMA-L list, I sent e-mail to listserv@american.edu with this single line in the body of the message:

SUBSCRIBE CINEMA-L Nancy Capulet

To unsubscribe, just send e-mail to the administrative address with the body of your message containing the line:

UNSUBSCRIBE *listname YourFirstName YourLastName*

When preparing this section, I learned about the mailing list CINEMA-L, which I read about on Liszt's Web page.

This list is dedicated to the discussion
of all forms of cinema, in all its aspects.

Get more information about the mailing list by e-mailing listserv@american.edu with this single line in the body of the message:

info CINEMA-L

You can receive a general help file by sending e-mail to listserv@american.edu with this single line in the body of the message:

help

Chat Rooms

Many matchmaking services now provide chat rooms for their
members. When you're in a chat room, which is like a conference room where participants can speak at any time, you can
type a message and hit the *return* key to display the text on
the screens of everyone in the chat room. Everyone can speak
at any time, but you have to push the *return* key to have what
you said broadcast to the other participants. Unlike e-mail, chat
is immediate. Like group discussions in the real world, you can
just listen, i.e., read; you don't need to talk, i.e., type responses.
Of course, some people may *lurk* in chat rooms—read without
writing anything.

Sometimes it can get difficult to follow a conversation or determine if someone's responding to your point or someone else's,
as you can see in this example:

STEAMER: I just finished the last of my finals!
           I'm ready to party!

GINGER: Hi ShyOne. Where are you from?

CAMILLA: You have little to lose and a lot to
           gain. You may only end up as friends.
           You could do worse by being alone.

SPICY: I'm ready to party too! Let's toast to
           the end of finals.

In addition to public chat rooms, where anyone is welcome,
many services also allow you to create or enter a private chat
room, which require a password. Private chat rooms are useful
for talking to a select group. Most often, they're used by two
people to have an intimate conversation.

If you want to write to a particular person in a chat room,
be careful not to broadcast your private message to the entire

room. Many *newbies*[2] broadcast intimate messages before they are aware of what capabilities are available and how they work. It's best to be familiar with how things work in a chat room before you send a confidential message. If you suspect someone is a newbie, consider sending instructions on how to send a private message along with your message.

With private messaging, you can write a message to a single individual. Private messaging is useful for inviting a particular individual to a private chat room. Like lots of women, when I first entered a chat room, I was bombarded with private messages.

Many of the services allow you to find out about those in the chat room. You may read their profiles or some words that they have written about themselves.

Chat rooms allow you to interact with like-minded people, or at least people who found the name of the chat room appealing. Chat rooms are great for people who like to interact in real-time with several people simultaneously. Participants tend to fire off responses, typing them quickly, so discussions can be filled with typos. However, you get a good sense of who people are since they tend to write what's currently on their minds.

Personally, I'm not a fan of chat rooms. People tend to write more coherently when given more time. That's why I prefer reading profiles, e-mail, and newsgroups.

Pitfalls

Just as in the physical world, there are people who will try to mislead you. They include:

- People posing as someone else.

- Con artists looking to trick you into giving them money, credit card numbers, or material possessions.

---

[2]The word *newbie* is originally from British public-school and military slang for "new boy." It is a neophyte, novice, or newcomer.

- Married people posing as single and available.
- Children pretending to be adults.

Be cautious when dealing with a stranger. Use common sense. You may encounter people, typically men, who want more attention, so they pose as women. Fortunately, many people who use chat rooms are exactly who they say they are.

Appendix C

Response Tracking

For those of you—typically women—who are bombarded with responses, I offer tips on how to keep track of your contacts and the status of your dialogues.

With the sheer quantity of responses I've received, I find it difficult to keep people straight. One time I sent a note to Tim and got an e-mail back informing me that his name was actually Kevin. I apologized for being so flaky. He said "It's okay. If we hit it off, we already have a pet name."

Fortunately, or unfortunately, I'm not the only one to have made this mistake. One guy addressed me as Gail. Another guy asked my friend Lisa, "How long have you been competing in ice skating tournaments?" She told him that she had never ice skated in her life.

I've sometimes told a man about my having lived in France only to have him interrupt and inform me that I already told him about it when we last spoke. I wish I could remember what I tell to my dates so I wouldn't appear so absent-minded. I keep all the e-mail I send, but up until I started writing this Appendix, I hadn't maintained records on my conversations. Like a therapist, maybe I should keep notes on my interactions and review them before our meeting. But how should I organize them?

I asked a couple of friends who had searched avidly for part-

ners what they do to keep track of their contacts and potential
dates. Few keep as meticulous records as Rosanne, Florence,
Tom, and Lisa, who rarely, if ever, commit the social blunders
that I have.

Taking Notes

Rosanne considered dating a numbers game. She figured she
would have to meet lots of people to find one that would be
right for her. Wanting to receive lots of responses, she placed no
distance restriction. She was open to meeting men from anywhere
in the world. Men wrote to her from Greenland, New Delhi, Peru,
as well as from all over the United States. She invited them to
have lunch with her when they visited San Francisco and a few
took her up on the offer. She frequently had business trips to
New York City and arranged meetings when she was there.

Rosanne used her office computer after-hours to pick up and
respond to her personal e-mail. She logged on after 5:30 P.M.
Often she was still in the office after 7 P.M. corresponding with
her new cyberbuddies. To keep track of them, she printed out
their profiles and e-mail. She kept a separate folder for each man.
When she spoke with someone on the telephone, she jotted down
notes on the back of his profile. Within three months of putting
her profile online, in addition to meeting Josh, with whom she
now lives, Rosanne had accumulated a stack of profiles and e-mail
about a foot and a half high.

Using a Database

Florence took online dating seriously. She put herself out there,
listing her profile on several different services. She didn't wait
for men to contact her; she initiated contact. To keep track of
men who responded, she set up a database in which she recorded
the following information:

Person's handle
Status (hot, lukewarm, dead)
Correspondence (messages sent and received)
First contact, who made it and when
Latest date Florence wrote
Latest date he wrote back
Need to respond?
Matchmaking service
Personal information
    Real name
    E-mail address
    Home town

From time to time, Florence analyzed the information in her database. Checking e-mail addresses, Florence occasionally discovered that a man wrote to her from two different services. She checked from which services she received the most interesting responses and pulled her ad off the others. Her database was a wonderful resource for keeping track of approximately 350 men with whom she has corresponded with over the course of a year.

Keeping Multiple Files

As I mentioned in Chapter 6, page 82, Tom designed his own searching tools. He was more meticulous about responding to women's ads than any man I've met. He replied quickly and he seemed to remember everything they had told him. He never repeated himself and he followed up when a woman failed to respond to his e-mail.

How did he keep everyone straight? He maintained three types of files. In the contact file, he stored contact information for each person with whom he corresponded, including her handle and any of the following information she had provided: real name, e-mail address, home and work telephone numbers, residential address, work address, directions, and places where they had been together.

In the correspondence file, he kept track of the status of all his online interaction. When he wrote to a woman, to the right of her handle, he placed a *W* to signify that he was *waiting* for a response. After he *received* a response, he changed their status to *R*, to indicate that he owed them a reply. If someone *contacted* him, he put a *C* to the right of the handle. Once he *met* a person, he wrote *M* to the right of their handle.

In his status file, he maintained notes on how he felt about someone—*no chemistry, no match* (when someone told him that she didn't feel they match), *taken* when the person was dating someone else or not available, and *possible* when he felt that there was potential for a relationship. If he discovered that he had already contacted the person using a different handle, then to the right of the handle, he put *Dup*, for duplicate, followed by the person's other handle(s). In addition to this information, Tom keeps notes on the looks, politics, and interests of his contacts.

Tom stored all e-mail messages from people with whom he corresponded, one file per person. Just before he met someone, he reviewed the person's entry in his status file and their e-mail correspondence.

Maintaining Spreadsheets

Within twelve hours of signing up for an online matchmaking service, Lisa received a half dozen responses. And responses kept flowing in, which surprised her since she didn't expect that many men would be interested in a forty-five year-old atheist who has children living with her.

Without faces and voices, she found it difficult to keep everyone straight. So she put together a system to keep track of all her responses—more than three dozen—using spreadsheets. Her system reminds me of methods used for keeping track of potential

Handle:

Name	Age	Date of Contact
Home Telephone	Birthday	Date Answered
Residence City	# Miles	Education
Work Telephone	Company	Photo online?
Work City	Profession	Body Type
E-mail	Ethnicity	Looks
# Kids	Religion	Height

Politics:

Self-Description:

Personality:

Red Flags:

Good Qualities

First Impression

Table C.1: Contact information and first impressions.

employers by those who are looking for a job.

Lisa maintained a separate spreadsheet, divided into three parts, for each person who contacts her. The top section, shown in Table C.1 on this page, is devoted mainly to factual information, contact information, appearance, and how a man feels about himself. This information helped her remember a person. Lisa also wrote down impressions when she received their first e-mail and read their profile. She left a few extra lines so that she can add other information.

Lisa used the middle section of her spreadsheet, shown in Table C.2 on the next page, for giving her ideas for conversation

| Favorite movies: |
| Plays, performances: |
| Fiction read: |
| Nonfiction: |
| Foreign Languages: |
| Schools Attended: |
| Grew up where: |
| Traveled where: |
| Hobbies and Interests: |
| Indoor Activities: |
| Outdoor Activities: |
| Comments: |
| |
| |

Table C.2: Topics for conversations.

and keeping track of what she learned and shared. She made comments about what she said, so that she wouldn't repeat the same funny hiking story over and over to the same person. She also kept notes on what they told her.

Many people who are looking for a match want to see whether the other person shares any of their interests and activities. Lisa saw such things as topics to discuss, but she felt it was much more important to find out how a man has treated people close to him, since she figures that he will probably treat her similarly. Does the person have a drinking or drug problem? Has he been involved in domestic violence? She devoted the bottom third of the spreadsheet, shown in Table C.3 on the facing page, to such information. She didn't usually find such things out on the first few dates.

While she was getting to know a person via e-mail, she would print out their messages and paper-clip them to the spreadsheet. She filed the spreadsheets in folders called "owe" (to remind her

Personal Information

Parents, their relationship
Ex-wives/girlfriend: current relationship
Relationship to mother
Relationship to father
Siblings
Relationship with children
How often family moved
Drinking habits
Drugs
Sex drive
Learned from mistakes
Lifestyle & goals

Table C.3: Relationship and character information.

that she owes them a response). Once she had written to them, she filed them in folders labeled "don't owe." When she wasn't interested in a person, she would file their paperwork in a folder labeled "rejects."

After Lisa met someone, she found she would no longer need to keep up the spreadsheet, once she has a face and real person to connect with the data.

Exercise: Useful Information

Writing this chapter made me think about what information I would like to review before meeting someone. If I were still searching for a mate online, I would consider recording the information shown in Table C.4 on the next page. What information would help you in your search for a mate?

Names
    Handle
    Real name
Status (hot, lukewarm, dead)
Addresses
    Matchmaking service
    E-mail address
    Home location
    Work location
    Where he's lived and traveled
Dates
    Dates he contacted me (e-mail, telephone, or in person)
    Dates I contacted him (e-mail, telephone, or in person)
    Age/birthday
Telephones
    Home telephone
    Work telephone
Appearance
    Photograph
    Height, weight or body type
    Hair (color, length, texture)
    Notable features (glasses, facial hair, type of clothing)
Relationships
    Relationship status: single, divorced, widowed
    Children
Hobbies/interests
Occupation
Comments

Table C.4: Information Nancy wishes she had kept.

Appendix D

Bibliography

I have divided this bibliography into four sections: (1) books on dating, (2) books on using personal ads, (3) books on computers, the Internet, and the Web, and (4) Web resources.

Dating

Atwood, Nina. *Be Your Own Dating Service: A Step-by-Step Guide to Finding and Maintaining Healthy Relationships* (Henry Holt, 1996)

> This excellent book offers exactly what its title suggests.

Cole, Judy. *Playing for Keeps: Dating, Seducing, & (maybe) Marrying the Modern Man* (Adams Media, 1997)

> This well-written book has many great tips for building your self-confidence and for dating in the modern world, where women no longer have to wait for Prince Charming to ask them out.

De Angelis, Barbara. *Are You the One for Me? Knowing Who's Right & Avoiding Who's Wrong* (Dell, 1992)

A useful book for helping you assess whether you are compatible with those whom you meet and date.

De Angelis, Barbara. *The Real Rules: How to Find the Right Man for the Real You* (Dell, 1997)

> Barbara De Angelis, like many others, thought that Ellen Fein and Sherrie Schneider's book *The Rules: Time-tested Secrets for Capturing the Heart of Mr. Right* didn't contain advice that would help readers capture men's hearts. So she wrote *The Real Rules*, with a more sensible set of rules, in my opinion.

Dominitz, Ben. *How to Find The Love of Your Life: A Step-By-Step Program that Really Works!* (Prima Publishing, 1985)

> Realizing that strategies for developing new business contacts can be applied to finding the love of your life, Ben Dominitz wrote this book after one of his business clients asked for suggestions on finding someone to love.

Gallatin, Martin. *Lover Shopping for Men & Women* (Pocket Books, 1987)

> A guide packed with amusing cartoons and great tips.

Giler, Janet Z. with Kathleen Neumeyer. *Redefining Mr. Right: A Career Woman's Guide to Choosing a Mate* (New Harbinger Publications, Inc., 1992)

> This book offers pointers on how to get involved in a lasting relationship.

Gosse, Richard. *You Can Hurry Love: An Action Guide for Singles Tired of Waiting* (Marin Publications, 1997)

This book explains how to get positive results in singles clubs, dating services, personal ads, websites, classes, and social events.

Gosse, Richard. *Singles Guide to the San Francisco Bay Area: Where and How to Meet a Romantic Partner and New Friends* (Marin Publications, 1997)

A guide to singles clubs, dating services, and publications in the San Francisco Bay Area.

Kahn, Elayne J. and David Rudnitsky. *Love Codes: How to Decipher Men's Secret Signals about Romance*

This guide will help you interpret signals a man is sending.

Kuriansky, Judy. *The Complete Idiot's Guide to Dating* (Alpha Books 1996)

Although the title makes this book sound lame, this book offers helpful advice. I highly recommend it.

Millman, Paul and the guys. *Buy Book, Get Guy* (Perigee, 1997)

An entertaining and informative book in which Paul Millman, and several other men, share insights from their years of dating. They reveal mistakes women commonly make and give "surefire" ways to meet and enchant the man of your dreams.

Page, Susan. *If I'm So Wonderful, Why Am I Still Single?* (Bantam Book, 1989)

Read this superb and friendly book if you want to answer the question in the title. It includes exercises and ten strategies that will change your love life forever.

Sills, Judith. *How to Stop Looking for Someone Perfect and Find Someone to Love* (Ballantine Books, 1984)

> If you want to meet that certain someone and settle in for the long-term, but you can't find anyone good enough for you, read this book. It describes just what its title says.

Tucker, Nita with Randi Moret.[1] *How Not to Stay Single: 10 Steps to A Great Relationship* (Crown Trade Paperbacks, 1996)

> This is an excellent results-oriented guide offering helpful hints and motivational thoughts on how to get into a great and lasting relationship.

Wingo, John and Julie. *At Long Last Love* (Warner Books, 1994)

> This warm, witty, but realistic book is filled with illuminating case histories from J. Wingo International, an introduction service. The book also includes exercises to help you assess yourself and your situation.

Wolf, Sharyn. *Guerrilla Dating Tactics: Strategies, Tips, and Secrets for Finding Romance* (Plume, 1994)

> If you are ready to go on the offensive, this guide is for you.

Placing Personal Ads

Beakman, Claudia and Karla Dougherty. *Playing The Personals: The Definitive Guide to Dating in the Nineties* (Pocket Books, 1996)

---

[1] When I attended the Sundance Film Festival in 1997, I met someone who told me that Randi Moret is a pen name and an anagram—two words formed by transposing the letters in her name.

A great guide for placing and responding to print personal ads—those found in the newspaper and magazines.

Digregorio, Charlotte. *Your Original Personal Ad: The Complete Guide to Expressing Your Unique Sentiments to Find Your Dream Person* (Civetta Press, 1995)

This book contains dozens of sample original ads, as well as lists of useful phrases and enticing words.

Hale, Mary. *Nice Girls Can, Men Can, Too: Personal Ads, Your Guide to Success A Career Woman's Approach* (Talking Hearts Press, 1995)

In this book, the author tells how she met her spouse through personal ads and gives you pointers so that you can follow in her footsteps.

Hinckley, Kathy and Peter Hesse. *Plain Fat Chick Seeks Guy Who Likes Broccoli: Humorous Personal Ads Written by Real People* (Gibbs Smith, 1997)

Real funny ads that Kathy Hinckley collected. This book might give you ideas if you are interested in writing your own humorous ad.

Using Computers, the Internet, and the Web

Krol, Ed and Bruce C. Klopfenstein, *The Whole Internet User's Guide & Catalog* (O'Reilly, 1996)

This was one of the first books published about the Internet and the Web and it continues to be one of the most popular.

Levine, John, Margaret Levine Young, and Arnold Reinhold. *Internet for Dummies* (IDG Books World Wide, 1997)

A thorough reference to the Internet.

Levine, John, Margaret Levine Young, and Arnold Reinhold. *Internet for Dummies Quick Reference* (IDG Books World Wide, 1997)

A compact yet thorough reference to the Internet.

Raymond, Eric S. (compiler). *The New Hacker's Dictionary* (IDG Books World Wide, 1996)

The author seems to have great fun compiling this guide to jargon and slang used online.

Finding Information on the Web

Advice for Online Personals

The Straight FAQ by Dean Esmay,
http://www.syndicomm.com/straight-faq.htm,
size 96K, 29-Jul-97.

Meyers-Briggs

Meyers Briggs FAQ–A Summary of Personality Typing
http://www-scf.usc.edu/~kanaris/faq-mbti.html,
size 29K, 20-Jul-95.

Etiquette

Wadham College E-Mail Etiquette,
http://www.wadham.ox.ac.uk/~jan/etiquette.html,
size 7K, 7.Apr.96.

E-Mail Etiquette,
http://www.nhmfl.gov/csg/helpdesk/mail/sect5-2-6.html,
size 887 bytes, 21.May.97.

E-Mail Etiquette,
http://www.howtoweb.com/email/emailetq.htm,
size 3K, 10.Mar.97.

Walden University—E-Mail Etiquette,
http://www.waldenu.edu/it/emaileti.html,
size 5K, 19.Nov.96.

Network Etiquette—for E-Mail and Newsgroups,
http://gps0.leeds.ac.uk/ucs/rules/etiquette.html,
size 7K, 24.Sep.96.

Yvain's guide to e-mail etiquette,
http://www.queer.org.au/qrd/net/guides/email-
etiquette.html, size 10K, 4.Oct.96.

E-Mail Etiquette,
http://www.net/es/netjunk/netikit.htm,
size 3K, 14.Mar.96.

Glossaries

Deja News,
http://www.dejanews.com/info/glossary.shtml.

Howe, Denis. *Free On-Line Dictionary Of Computing (FOLDOC),*
wombat.doc.ic.ac.uk/foldoc/index.html, 9K, 8.Dec.97.

Raymond, Eric S. *The Jargon File,*
http://www.monmouth.com/~jshahom/jargon.

Appendix E

Glossary

Here is a glossary of terms that are used in this guide. Following the term, I have sometimes included its pronunciation in between two slashes, for example, /ee-moh'ti-kon/. The context where the word is typically used and its plural form are given in square brackets, for example, [Usenet]. Abbreviations, long-hand notation, and etymology are enclosed in parentheses, for example, (IDG). I have indicated the type of word it is, with n. for noun, v. for verb, adj. for adjective, and adv. for adverb.

AA n. Alcoholics Anonymous is an organization that helps people to overcome their addiction to alcohol.

anonymous e-mail n. E-mail in which the sender's identity is concealed. With systems that support anonymous e-mail, a message isn't sent directly to you. Instead, it's sent to the *handle* you use for the dating service, and then forwarded to you electronically. Anonymous e-mail addresses are often available through online matchmaking services. They are also available through some e-mail services, for example, hotmail (`www.hotmail.com`). Note, Hotmail now asks for your real name (but you can make up a false one).

article n. A message posted to an *Internet discussion group*.

ASCII /aˈss-(,)kee/ (American Standard Code for Information Interchange) Plain text on a computer, typically using a fixed-width font, such as `Courier`.

automated agent n. A system that sends you an automatic notification when a person meets your criteria.

BBS (Bulletin Board System) n. A computer and associated software that typically provides an electronic message database where people can log in and leave messages. Messages are often split into topic groups similar to the newsgroups on Usenet. Any user may submit or read any message in these public domain areas.

browser [World Wide Web] n. A program that allows a person to read Web pages. Netscape Navigator, Internet Explorer, Mosaic, and Lynx are examples of browsers.

chat v. When two or more people have an online real-time conversation typically via a network.

chat room n. A virtual room in cyberspace where you can communicate in real time with the other occupants. Chat rooms are like conference calls: Participants type their message, the text is displayed as soon as they hit the *return* key and after any other text that has been queued up has been typed on the screen.

ciphertext n. Text that has been encrypted by an encryption system.

commercial online service (COS) n. Companies that offer online access, such as America Online (AOL), CompuServe, and Prodigy. They typically provide discussion groups (sometimes known as forums), chat rooms, e-mail, online events, and Internet Access. Here are their telephone numbers:

Service	Phone Numbers
America Online (AOL)	800-827-6364; 703-448-8700
CompuServe	800-848-8990; 614-718-2800
Prodigy	800-776-3449; 914-448-8000
Microsoft Network (MSN)	800-386-5550
Delphi	800-695-4005; 617-441-4801

cyberspace /si'ber-spays/ n. A term used to describe the virtual place where people meet when they encounter one another on the Internet.

debug v. Attempt to determine the cause of some unexpected results.

digest n. A periodic collection of messages that have been posted to a *newsgroup* or *mailing list.* A digest is prepared by a *moderator* who rejects inappropriate submissions, formats the articles, and adds a contents list. The digest is then either mailed to the *mailing list* or posted to the *newsgroup.*

discussion group n. See *Internet Discussion Group.*

directory n. A hierarchical catalog of the Web. Directories are like subject card catalogs that used to be in our libraries before they were computerized. The directory contents are broken down to topics and subtopics. Here are URLs for some popular Web directories:

Excite!	`www.excite.com`
Infoseek	`www.infoseek.com`
Lycos	`www.lycos.com`
Yahoo!	`www.yahoo.com`

Search engines, like directories, can also assist you in finding what you want on the Web.

electronic token n. An electronic document issued as currency for payment of goods and services sold over the Internet.

e-mail or **email** n. (singular or plural) An electronically transmitted message (or messages) that is typically sent from
  one computer user to one or more other users, often through
  computer networks or via modems over telephone lines.

e-mail verification Some systems verify your e-mail address by
  sending you a message to which you reply, or you log in
  to their service using information they provided in their
  e-mail message to you. This authentication verifies that
  your e-mail address is what you claim it to be; it protects
  against someone impersonating you.

emoticon /ee-moh′ti-kon/ n. Also known as *smiley*. ASCII
  characters that convey information nonverbally to indicate
  an emotional state in e-mail or messages. Originally mostly
  used to indicate something is intended in jest.

  Hundreds of emoticons have been proposed, but only a few
  are in common use. These include:

  :-) or :) A smiley face often used to indicate humor,
    laughter, friendliness, and occasionally sarcasm.

  ;-) or ;) A winking smiley face.

  :-(or :(A frown or sad face for sadness, anger, or dis-
    content.

  For best viewing of these faces, tilt your head to the left.

  --<--<--@ A rose.

encryption n. Any procedure used to convert *plaintext* into *ciphertext* in order to prevent any but the intended recipient
  from reading that message or data. PGP is an encryption
  program available for free, see page 171.

f2f adj. An abbreviation for *face to face*.

face to face adj. Meet in person as opposed to meeting on the Net.

FAQ /F-A-Q/ or /fak/ [Usenet] n. Frequently Asked Questions. A compendium of lore, accumulated by an expert familiar with a topic, often posted periodically to high-volume newsgroups in an attempt to forestall frequently or commonly asked questions. One such example is Dean Esmay's *The Straight FAQ*, which he regularly posts to the newsgroup `alt.personals`. It can be found on the Web at `http://www.syndicomm.com/straight-faq.html`.

flame v. To post or e-mail a nasty message intended to insult and provoke.

forum n. [plural fora or forums] Any discussion group accessible through a dial-in BBS, a mailing list, or a newsgroup. A forum functions much like a bulletin board; users submit postings for all to read and discussion ensues.

GUI Graphical User Interface.

handle n. (From CB slang.) A code name or pseudonym; a "nom de guerre" intended to conceal the user's true identity. Handles function as the same sort of simultaneous concealment and display one finds on Citizen's Band radio, from which the term was adopted.

hard disk [storage] n. A magnetic disk used to store data, i.e., files, folders, and directories, on your computer. Computers usually have at least one hard disk permanently connected to the computer. Some computers have removable disks.

header n. The part of an e-mail message or discussion group article that precedes the body and contains, among other things, the sender's name and e-mail address or handle and the date the message was sent.

hierarchy n. The first part of a newsgroup name, for example, `rec` is the hierarchy of the newsgroup `rec.food.recipes`.

hit [World Wide Web] n. A request for a Web page. Typically this term is used when describing the activity of a Web site, e.g., The Hearts Online Web site got over 3,000 hits on February 14, 1998.

home page [World Wide Web] n. The top-level Web page on a site typically relating to an individual or institution. Find Hearts Online's home page at `www.HeartsOnline.com`. Other pages on a server are usually accessible by following links from the home page.

hot list n. Use a hot list to keep track of the people who interest you. You can also use it to keep track of people to whom you've sent e-mail.

HTML (HyperText Markup Language) /H-T-M-L/ [World Wide Web] n. This language is used to specify the format and content of Web pages.

hypertext n. A term coined by Ted Nelson around 1965 for a collection of documents (or *nodes*) containing cross-references or *links* that, with the aid of an interactive browser program, allow the reader to move easily from one document to another.

IDG n. See *Internet Discussion Group*.

instant message n. A message that is transmitted instantly (in real-time) to a designated person currently online, often used for inviting a particular individual to a private chat room.

Internet (Net) n. A huge collection of computers all around the world that are connected. Internet users can send messages and information from one computer to another.

Internet Discussion Group (IDG) /I-D-G/ n. The primary
method for group communication on the Internet, IDGs
include Usenet newsgroups, mailing lists, corporate discussion groups, and IRC (Internet Relay Chat). Deja News
archives IDGs.

ISP (Internet Service Provider) n. ISPs do what their name implies: they provide service or access to the Internet. There
are many listings of ISPs. One such listing can be found at
www.internet.com, in which they are listed by area code
and country code.

link n. When you're connected to the Web, you click on highlighted text—a *link*—and your browser gathers more information (which may be stored halfway around the world on
a different Web page). Your browser then displays it. It is
these many links that make this collection of information
behave like a web.

list server or **Listserv** n. An automatic mailing list server.

LOL also **lol** Short for Laugh Out Loud. People use *LOL* to
indicate if something is intended to be funny. People also
use it as a reply to indicate that something made them
laugh out loud.

Lynx /links/ n. Lynx is a character-based browser for viewing text on Web sites. It receives files much faster than
graphic-oriented browsers, such as Netscape Navigator or
Internet Explorer, because Lynx only displays text or ascii
characters. Other browsers display graphics and text.

mailing list n. A collection of computer users to whom a message is sent. Most mailing lists just forward e-mail sent to
the list. Others are filtered by humans or programs; lists
edited or filtered by humans are called *moderated.*

mail server n. A computer program that distributes files or information in response to requests sent via electronic mail. Electronic mailing lists are often maintained by a mail server.

match n. A person who meets your desired search criteria. See also *two-way match*.

mensch n. (From Yiddish.) A person of integrity and honor.

MFA n. Master of Fine Arts.

moderated adj. Submissions to a newsgroup or a mailing list that are edited or filtered by a human.

modem n. A device connected to a computer, workstation, or terminal that enables data to be transfered using a telephone line.

Net n. An abbreviation for the Internet.

netiquette /net'i-ket/ n. Network etiquette. Conventions of politeness specific to the Internet.

netnews /net'n[y]ooz/ n. The content of Usenet.

newbie [jargon] /n[y]oo'bee/ n. (Originally from British public-school and military slang variant of "new boy.") A neophyte, novice, or newcomer.

newsgroup [Usenet] (see also Internet Discussion Groups) n. One of Usenet's huge collection of topic groups or forums. Usenet groups can be *unmoderated* (anyone can post) or *moderated* (submissions are automatically directed to a moderator, who edits or filters and then posts the results). Some moderated groups are distributed as *digests*, with groups of postings periodically collected into a single large posting with an index.

news reader n. A browser program that enables a user to read articles posted to Usenet. You can read news using Internet Explorer, Netscape Navigator, trn (on Unix systems), GNUS, and nn.

online classifieds n. Ads in cyberspace that are similar to classifieds in the newspaper.

online dating service n. A service that provides specific information about its members.

online matchmaking service n. A service that, in addition to listing information about its members, also provides tools for finding members who meet a user's specifiable criteria.

PC Short for politically correct or personal computer.

plaintext n. A message before it's encrypted or after it's decrypted, that is, in its usual form, which anyone can read, as opposed to its encrypted form (*ciphertext*).

PGP (Pretty Good Privacy) n. A program for encrypting a message so that only the intended recipient can read it, see page 171.

profile n. A profile consists of personal information such as age, gender, religion, and height, for other members of a matchmaking service to view.

RAM [storage] n. Random Access Memory. Fast memory used by a computer, as opposed to *hard disk* space, which takes longer for a computer to access.

real time adv. In jargon, refers to doing something live or at the present time. A telephone enables you to communicate in real time. Users communicate in real time in chat rooms.

search engine [World Wide Web] n. A remotely accessible program, i.e., it runs on another computer on the Internet, that
lets you search for information on the Internet. You can use
a search engine to look up documents on the Web. For a
brief description of search engines, see page 174. Here are
some of the most popular search engines:

AltaVista	`www.altavista.digital.com`
Dogpile	`www.dogpile.com`
Excite!	`www.excite.com`
Hotbot	`www.hotbot.com`
Infoseek	`www.infoseek.com`
Lycos	`www.lycos.com`
Metacrawler	`www.metacrawler.com`
Webcrawler	`www.webcrawler.com`
Yahoo!	`www.yahoo.com`

You can find matchmaking sites on the Internet by searching for words such as: *dating, matchmaking* or *matchmakers, personals, romance,* and *singles.*

smiley n. See *emoticon.*

snail mail n. (From "US Mail" via "USnail.") Paper mail sent
via the postal service as opposed to electronic mail. A
postal address is, correspondingly, a "snail mail address."

spam v. (From the Monty Python *Spam* song.) To post messages to newsgroups or send e-mail that's irrelevant, inappropriate, or unsolicited and unwanted, e.g., get-rich-quick
schemes, pointers to sex sites, and chain letters.

surfing the Web v. Wandering around the World Wide Web
looking for interesting things.

tantra yoga Yoga with a sexual orientation.

token See *electronic token.*

two-way match n. A match in which two people meet each other's criteria. Consider, for example, Jenny, who is thirty-four years old, slim, and wants to meet a man who is betweeen thirty-three and thirty-nine years old, and Jim, who is thirty-eight years old and wants to meet a woman who is between thirty and thirty-eight and not overweight. They would be considered compatible on a system that provides two-way matching.

UC Berkeley University of California at Berkeley.

unmoderated adj. Submissions in a newsgroup or mailing list that are unfiltered and posted exactly how they are sent.

URL (Universal Resource Locator) /U-R-L/ [World Wide Web] n. A standard for specifying an object on the Internet, such as a file or newsgroup. URLs are used extensively on the World Wide Web. They are also used in HTML documents to specify the target of a hyperlink.

Here are some example of URLs:

```
http://www.HeartsOnline.com
mailto:capulet@HeartsOnline.com
news:alt.personals
```

The letters or words before the first colon specifies the access scheme or protocol. The letters or words after the colon is interpreted according to the access scheme. In general, two slashes after the colon introduce a hostname (host:port is also valid). Schemes include: `http` (World Wide Web), `ftp` (file transfer protocol), and `gopher`. Other less commonly used schemes include: `news`, `telnet`, and `mailto` (e-mail).

Usenet /yooz'net/ n. (From "Users' Network.") A vast system of discussion groups called newsgroups on a variety of topics. A discussion group is essentially a bulletin board in cyberspace containing messages from people all around the world.

verification, e-mail n. See *e-mail verification.*

virtual adj. Commonly refers to artificial objects created by a computer system. For example, a *chat room* is not a room, but within it there are interactions like those that would take place in a room in the physical world.

white pages n. An online directory service for finding someone's address (analogous to a telephone directory). See page 176. The white pages directory services on the Internet include:

Four11	`www.four11.com`
Switchboard	`www.switchboard.com`
WhoWhere	`www.whowhere.com`

World Wide Web n. Also known as the Web, WWW, and W3, is a collection of information stored on computers world wide. If you have a computer, a reading program (called a browser), an Internet account, you connect to your Internet account, log on, start your browser, give it a Web address—such as `www.HeartsOnline.com`—and start reading.

WYSIWYG /wiz'ee-ayg/ adj. Short for *What You See is What You Get.* Typically used to describe a friendly user interface, in which you get immediate visual feedback.

Credits: Entries in this glossary were compiled from The Jargon File, the Free On-Line Dictionary Of Computing (FOLDOC), the Deja News Glossary, and *The Internet for Dummies Quick Reference.*

Appendix F

Survey of Matchmaking Sites

This Appendix surveys a few online matchmaking services. A side-by-side comparison is listed in the table on page 232.

Match.com (www.match.com)

Match.com held focus groups to determine what would make women sign up for an online matchmaking service. Then they used this information to design their system. The founders realized that if women signed up, men would also join. The founders thought about what would make women feel comfortable, what women would like to know and what they would be willing to reveal about themselves. For example, Match.com doesn't ask for your weight. Instead it asks your body type and gives you a choice of slim/slender, average, athletic, a few extra pounds, large, other, and prefer not to say.

Match.com is committed to providing a safe community. It doesn't allow crude language or sexually explicit material. If you violate their policies, they'll hide your profile from other members.

The site was designed to appeal to professional single adults. Their monthly fee, which is roughly $10, intentionally serves as a screen.

Match.com asks about you and your desired match. Questions include your and your desired match's ethnicity, religion, body type, height, smoking and drinking habits, number of children and plans for having children, and the distance you're willing to look for a match. The computer uses this information to find matches for you. Additionally, you're asked for a handle, a headline, and a description that can be up to 2000 characters in length. If you want, you may provide a photograph. Members and guests may browse this information. Figure F.1 on the next page shows a profile from Match.com.

Search Capabilities

Match.com provides several tools for searching their database:

- *Handle Search* — To find a specific member (like someone who has contacted you).

- *Browse* — To search a specific region of the country for:
  All Men
  Men Seeking Women
  Men Seeking Men
  All Women
  Women Seeking Men
  Women Seeking Women

- *Power Browse* — To be more selective for whom you're looking. In addition to providing the capabilities of browse, with power browse you can specify an age range, one or more ethnicities and/or religions. You can also see all profiles or those that have been placed or updated in the last two days, week, two weeks, month, two months, or since you last logged into Match.com. With this capability you can view just active members.

Handle: Garten
Headline: Seeking a bright, independent woman.

34 year-old male, located in Berkeley, seeking 22 to
42 year-old female for long-term relationship.

I'm bright, honest, independent, thoughtful, affectionate,
sometimes funny, sometimes serious, sometimes quiet,
sometimes opinionated, sometimes confident, sometimes
shy.   I like reading almost anything: history, current
nonfiction, popular science, liberal politics, feminist
theory, literature, science fiction, newspapers, book
reviews, news and opinion and literary magazines,
technical and computing publications.   (A few favorites:
The Dispossessed by Ursula K. Le Guin, _A Perfect Vacuum_
by Stanislaw Lem, _Lord Jim_ by Joseph Conrad.) I also
like new experiences and learning things that one can't
learn from books.   I enjoy the theater (especially classic
plays), bridge and board games, public radio, traveling and
exploring new places and old favorites, eating out. I'm thin
but fit, and I would enjoy sharing exercise or outdoor
activities (recently I have been bicycling in the Berkeley
hills and working out at the gym).   I'm financially secure
after several years in research; I'm currently back in
school finishing my PhD.   I'm looking for someone who
is bright, probably well educated, independent, honest,
someone whom I can talk to, who enjoys her work, who has
opinions about all sorts of things, and who is also looking
for a long-term relationship.

Profile:

Ethnicity:	Caucasian
Religion:	Atheist
Body Type:	Slim/slender
Height:	6 ft., 1 in. (185 cm)
Smoking:	Don't smoke
Drinking:	Drink socially/occasionally
Children:	Don't have children
Plans for Children:	Undecided

Profile of Desired Match:
Smoking: Doesn't smoke

Figure F.1: A Match.com profile.

- *Super Search* — To find people who meet specific criteria. In addition to providing the capabilities of power browse, with super search you can select based on type of relationship desired (e-mail pen-pal, activity partner, short-term relationship, long-term relationship), body type (slim/slender, average, athletic, a few extra pounds, or large), height, smoking and drinking habits, children status (doesn't have children, has children living with him or her, has children not living with him or her, or has children living with him or her sometimes), desire for children, and distance you live from another member.

In addition to online personal ads, Match.com provides tips, advice, a calendar of events, and an online magazine. Match.com also has chat rooms, whose features I describe in Appendix B on page 186.

Friend Finder (`www.friendfinder.com`)

Friend Finder requests much of the same information as Match.com. It requests physical information (sex, race, date of birth, height, body type), personal information (what type of relationship you're looking for, religion, education, smoking and drinking habits, number of children, and interest in having children), and geographical information (where you live and what languages you speak). I've included a profile from Friend Finder in Figure F.2 on the facing page. You can also fill in a personality profile to give other members a sense of your priorities.

Search Capabilities

You can search the profile database by race, gender, age, height, body type, religion, educational level, smoking and drinking habits, geographic location, and distance from your home. You can also look for ads with photographs and personality profiles. If you

Handle: BrightAndBold
Headline: By the Sea, By the Beautiful Sea

Fun-loving divorced woman with attractive face and figure, enjoys reading, quality conversation, Shakespeare, yoga, Bach, PBS, variety of art, mostly 19th century, hiking, canoeing, outdoors, and theater. I am a architect, play clarinet and make stained glass windows. Nonsmoker, light drinker.
 # Views: 8
Last Visit: 12/10/97

Ideal Person-looking for a loving, professional man who has a depth and sensitivity for the arts and culture, is educated and looking for a permanent relationship with no games, light smoking, light drinker and has a sense of humor. Pipe smoking ok.

P h y s i c a l	I n f o r m a t i o n
Gender	Female
Race	Caucasian
Born on	1951.4.12 (47 years old)
Height	5 ft 4 in
Body Type	Average
P e r s o n a l	**I n f o r m a t i o n**
Looking for	A man for a long term relationship or marriage.
Occupation	Architect
Religion	No response
Education	BA/BS (4 year degree)
Smoking/Drinking	I'm a nonsmoker
	I'm a light/social drinker
Has children?	Has children, not at home
Wants children?	No response
G e o g r a p h i c a l	**I n f o r m a t i o n**
Lives in	Evanston, Illinois, United States
Speaks	English

Figure F.2: A Friend Finder profile.

don't feel like searching, you can instead look at the list of recent "cool" profiles—profiles that the staff at Friend Finder consider interesting.

There's another way to look for people on Friend Finder: Tell them how you feel about a couple of members and then Friend Finder uses collaborative filtering to recommend other people to you. Here's how it works: Suppose you like Anna and Katie, Friend Finder searches their database and finds other people who also like Anna and Katie and recommends to you the people that those people like. For example, suppose Steve likes Anna, Katie, and Lisa, and Fred likes Anna, Katie, Karen, and Lisa. Then the system would recommend Lisa to you, since two other people who share your interest in Anna and Katie like Lisa also.

In addition to providing chat rooms and a relationship magazine, Friend Finder has an advice column, which resembles the discussion groups that I describe in Appendix B, page 178. You can pose a question and other members can post advice or indicate whether they agree or disagree with another members' response.

If you're looking for erotic partners, you might want to check out Adult Friend Finder (`adult.friendfinder.com`). The ratio of men to women on Adult Friend Finder is about ten to one. If you're looking for a sports or activity partner, then consider Sports & Games Friend Finder (`sports.friendfinder.com`).

Swoon (`www.swoon.com`)

Unlike Match.com and Friend Finder, Swoon is free. Personal ads are only a small part of the Swoon Web site. Swoon is designed to be an online supplement to Advance Publications, which includes magazines such as GQ, Details, Glamour, and Mademoiselle. Swoon was designed specifically for twentysomethings, though you don't need to be in your twenties to use it. "Swoon provides a place for users to interact, both with the site and with each other, through a variety of features, such as forums (discussion groups), games, chat, and personals," says Swoon Editor-in-Chief, Lamar Graham.

Although Swoon asks lots of questions, I found their questionnaire inviting because they hold your hand through the process and inject a bit of humor. They start by asking about your vital statistics, which includes your gender, the gender of whom you are seeking, your marital status, your birthday (which you can hide with the click of a button), your astrological sign (which you can also hide), your telephone area code or country code (which is used in searching), your ethnicity, your religion, your educational level, your occupation, your smoking, drinking and drug habits, your hair and eye color, your height, and your weight.

Unlike Match.com and Friend Finder, which present you with a blank space where you describe yourself and who you're looking for, Swoon poses specific questions. They invite you to "dazzle potential mates with your wit, your creativity, your attention to grammar and spelling" when filling in the following blanks:

> I've got _____in my CD player.
> The last book I read was _____.
> The last movie I saw was _____.
> The URLs of my three favorite web sites are
>   `http://`_____
>   `http://`_____
>   `http://`_____
> I'm an excellent lover because _____
> _____
> I'd be willing to get arrested over _____
> _____
> The best date I've ever had was _____
> _____
> The most unusual place I've ever made love was ___
> _____
> For kicks, I like to _____

Say something smart about yourself. _____

When asking for a headline, Swoon encourages you to "Write a short phrase that describes you and/or what you're looking for. You make your first impression with your headline, so be as intriguing, witty and revealing as you possibly can."

Swoon then asks what you're looking for in a partner, which gives you an opportunity to specify the marital status, age range, location (in terms of telephone area codes), ethnicity, religion, education, height, weight, hair color, and eye color of whom you are seeking. Your desires are included in your profile.

Search Capabilities

Swoon offers two types of searches: a Simple Search is designed to get the broadest possible results and an Advanced Search is for submitting a detailed query. Running a few searches in the San Francisco Bay Area, I determined the ratio of men to women using Swoon is about 2.5 to 1, which I subsequently learned, from an employee who works on Swoon, is about the ratio on their system overall.

With the Advanced Search, you can specify the height and weight of your desired match. I saw one man who stated that he wanted to meet a woman 5' to 5'10" whose weight is between 100 lbs and 130 lbs. I wonder whether he realizes that a woman who is 5' and 130 lbs may be a bit plump and a woman who is 5'10" and 100 lbs will look anorexic. The system does not allow him to specify a weight range for specific heights. Now I understand why some systems ask for your body type rather than your weight.

Goodcompany.com (www.goodcompany.com)

Goodcompany.com considers itself "an online social club where you can expand your circle of friends." It's designed to give people with Internet access a way to cultivate friendships, develop romantic relationships, find activity partners, travel companions, or simply friends with common interests.

Goodcompany.com asks about your favorite food, music, books, films, TV shows, sports or leisure activities, as well was what you like to do when you go out in the evening, the languages you speak, your dietary preferences, your pets, education level, marital status, if you have children, your height, body type, physical characteristics, ethnicity, religious or spiritual beliefs, time and place you were born, smoking and drinking habits, and your interest in traveling. They also pose a few essay questions:

- Of what historical event do you have the most vivid memories and why?

- Pretend I'm your personal genie. If you could ask one wish to be granted, what would it be?

- Where's your favorite place to get a cup of coffee and what makes that place so special? Don't drink coffee? Then describe your favorite neighborhood haunt.

- Tell us more about yourself. What do you do for a living? What's your dream occupation? What are your passions in life?

Goodcompany.com offers a variety of options to help members find people with common interests. A range of matching systems, based on everything from interests and hobbies to geographic location and languages spoken, gives members the opportunity to choose the criteria most important in finding new friends. Goodcompany.com provides a messaging system to notify members when other people who share their interests are online and where to find them. Their system is designed to help members to learn about other members' preferences, attitudes, values, and lifestyles and will recommend those with whom you are likely to be compatible.

Using goodcompany.com, you can communicate with other members via anonymous e-mail, instant messaging,[1] chat, or through a message board or discussion group.

JDate (www.jdate.com)

There are numerous sites whose focus is on religion. JDate is just one. After reading that online dating sites will be big business, Joe Shapira started JDate. JDate is dedicated to matching Jewish singles. In addition to online personal ads, JDate provides online chatting, streamed video and audio, and a bulletin board for members to express their feelings and opinions.

In addition to the usual vital statistics, JDate asks how often you go to synagogue and whether you keep kosher. They ask your educational level, the emphasis of your studies, your occupation, annual income (which you specify in a range or can opt not to say), where you grew up, and your smoking and drinking habits. They present thirty-five personality traits, which are listed in Table F.1 on the next page, and ask which ones you have. JDate also wants to know the languages you speak, your favorite activities, cuisine, music, and what you read. It asks you to describe the person you would like to meet in terms of age range, religious background, marital status, educational level, and smoking and drinking habits.

The service poses several essay questions and each answer can be at most 200 words long. It asks you to describe the person you would like to meet, a perfect date, your perceptions of an ideal relationship, and what you've learned from past relationships.

---

[1] An instant message is transmitted instantly (in real-time) to a designated person currently online.

Adventurous	Humorous	Shy
Argumentative	Intellectual	Simple
Artistic	Liberal	Sophisticated
CleanCut	Low Maintenance	Spiritual
Compulsive	Musical	Spontaneous
Conservative	Nurturing	Stubborn
Earthy	Practical	Talkative
Easygoing	Procrastinator	Unconventional
Eccentric	Quiet	Wild
Flexible	Romantic	Witty
High Energy	Sensitive	Worldly
High Maintenance	Serious	

Table F.1: JDate asks you to indicate which of these personality traits you have.

You can include up to five photographs of yourself. JDate has the sharpest (highest resolution) photographs of all the systems I have seen.

In addition to being able to search for members who meet certain criteria and live in a certain country or area code (you can specify up to five such codes), you can ask for members with photographs.

The information JDate presents is not only helpful for figuring out whether you share interests, goals, and lifestyle, but it's also great for striking up a conversation and deciding what to do on the first date.

Matchmaker (www.matchmaker.com)

Matchmaker is one of the oldest online matchmaking services. It was started in the late 1980s before the Web existed. Matchmaker consists of scores of sites that are closely networked. If you sign up with one service, you can do searches and browse profiles on any of their other sites. Each site is overseen by its own producer, who customizes the service to its members' specific needs.

Matchmaker has the most extensive questionnaire I have run across. Unlike many other systems, you can't browse their ads until you complete their questionnaire, which has around fifty multiple choice questions and about twenty essay questions. Their questions ask about your physical appearance as well as your personality and preferences. Here are a couple of the questions together with some of the alternatives offered:

You might best be described as:

> Intelligent/Driven
> Romantic/Optimistic
> Cheerful/Realistic
> Daring/Wild
> Quiet/Serene
> Naive/Sheltered
> Bleak/Moody
> Just plain stupid.

Where would you prefer to live? Possible responses include:

> A farm in the country
> A cottage in the country
> The heart of the city
> On a yacht in the Caribbean

Some of the questions are amusing, such as one which asks for your astrological sign, and offers "neon" and "stop" as possible choices. When asked to describe your television viewing habits, the alternatives include:

> It's on MTV and the knob is gone.
> I watch PBS exclusively.
> The Bugs Bunny/Road Runner Show.

You can only pick one, even if you watch more than one channel.

Here are a few sample questions from the essay section:

- If you were to inherit a fortune, what would you do with it?

- If you could change one thing about yourself, what would it be and why?

- If you were to meet someone for the first time, what would be the perfect setting?

- What would someone notice first about you?

- What are your lifelong goals? Where would you like to be tomorrow? Where would you like to be in two years? In five years?

Many members appreciate that there is lots of information about other people on the system, but their long questionnaire might scare people away.

When you search their database of members, the system reports what percentage of your answers are the same as the other person's. Your answers match with a high percentage when you have among other things, similar tastes in music, vacation spots, favorite colors, hair color. I don't care whether someone is not the same height or whether their favorite color is the same as mine, but I would like to meet someone who prefers living in a city to the country, who leads a lifestyle similar to mine, and who likes the types of food I do.

Matchmaker reports more statistics on its members than any other system I have seen. It indicates:

> when he signed up for the service,
> when he last logged in,
> how many times his profile has been browsed,
> how many messages he has received,
> and how many messages he has sent.

Such information is a great help in determining how active a member is, and whether she tends to initiate conversations by writing to other members.

Matchmaker includes over sixty sites. Some serve people who live in particular international and metropolitan areas; others cater to specialized groups such as teenagers, college students, people over 40, Christians, or Jews. The address of an individual site can usually be written www.*name*.matchmaker.com. In place of *name*, substitute the name of a specific service, e.g., christian, yenta, silicon, boston, or newyork.

Other Sites

New sites appear regularly. Some services grow out of frustration with other services. For example, the founders of Introducing.com (www.introducing.com), grew tired of Web sites filled with inactive members, so Introducing.com removes inactive people from their system.

Some sites are affiliated with other services, e.g., Webpersonals (www.webpersonals.com), is a sideline for Telepersonals, a telephone-based meeting service. Webpersonals offers key-word searching, enabling their members to search for ads that contain or don't contain a given word.

American Singles (www.as.org) was founded by Richard Gosse in 1978. Mr. Gosse is the author of several dating books including *You Can Hurry Love: An Action Guide for Singles Tired of Waiting* and *Singles Guide to the San Francisco Bay Area: Where and How to Meet a Romantic Partner and New Friends.*

RWR Technology founded several sites, including Singles Only (`www.singlesonly.com`), Single Jew (`www.singlejew.com`), and Christians Together (`www.christianstogether.com`). To encourage you to put your picture online, they will extend your membership when you send your photograph.

LoveHappens.com is based on technology and content developed by Match.com and Thrive. The Match.com (`www.match.com`) database of people and their matchmaking engine is available to users of LoveHappens.com. Thrive (`www.thriveonline.com`) provides content for the site, including advice, tips, polls of members opinions, message boards, quizzes, and articles on romance, dating, relationships, sexuality, and love.

Not only is Yahoo a search engine on the Web, but it provides classified ads (`classifieds.yahoo.com`), which include online personals.

Free Services

Free services tend to have many more members and a lot of them may not be as serious about meeting someone. Nevertheless, here are services that are 100 percent free:

American Singles	`www.as.org`
Classified2000	`www.classified2000.com`
Courtship Corner	`www.talkcity.com/courtship`
Date.com	`www.date.com`
Intermingle	`www.intermingle.com`
MeetMeOnline	`www.meetmeonline.com`
Swoon	`www.swoon.com`
Webpersonals	`www.webpersonals.com`
Yahoo! Classifieds	`classifieds.yahoo.com`

For a comparison of several matchmaking sites, see the table on page 232.

Feature/Service	Friend Finder	goodcompany	JDate	Match.com	Matchmaker	Swoon
URL, starts with www, ends with .com	friendfinder	goodcompany	jdate	match	matchmaker	swoon
Focus of Site	general	general	Jewish	general	general	age 20-30
Price	$0-$8.50	free in '98	$9-$13	$5-$13	$10	free
Date founded	early '96	1/98	4/97	1995	5/90	1996
E-mail Forwarded	yes	yes	yes	yes	no	yes
Profile						
Questionnaire size	short	medium	medium	short	long	medium
# multiple choice	14	16	32	17	50	27
# essay questions	1	4 + 16 short	5	1	15	7
Activity indication	yes	no	no	yes	yes	no
Photographs	yes	yes	up to 5	yes	yes	yes
Searching						
Distance	yes	yes	no	yes	yes	no
Area code	no	no	yes	no	no	yes
2-way matching	no	no	no	yes	no	no
Automated agent	yes	no	no	yes	no	no
Photos	yes	yes	yes	no	no	no
Hot list	yes	yes	no	no	yes	no
Additional features						
Chat	yes	yes	yes	yes	yes	yes
Discussion groups	no	yes	soon	no	no	yes
Online magazine	yes	yes	no	yes	no	yes
Calendar	no	yes	no	yes	no	no
Advice column	yes	yes	no	yes	no	yes

Index

ORDER FORM

I would like to order: *Putting Your Heart Online*
   Number of copies: _____ at \$18.95 each   _____
Sales Tax:
   California residents add 8.25% sales tax   _____
   New Jersey residents add 6% sales tax   _____
Shipping:
   Within North America   free
   Within the USA via Priority Mail   \$3/book
   Outside North America   \$7/book
                              Shipping _____
Payment   Total   _____
   ☐ Check enclosed in US dollars payable to Variable Symbols
   ☐ Credit card: ☐ AMEX ☐ MasterCard ☐ Visa
   Card number: _____
   Name on card: _____ Exp. date: __ /__
   Signature: _____
Ship to:
   Name: _____
   Address: _____
   _____
   City: _____ State: _____
   Zip: _____ Country: _____
   Phone: _____ Fax: _____
   E-mail: _____

E-mail or send orders to:

Variable Symbols, Inc.
33 Linda Avenue, Suite 2210
Oakland, CA 94611-4819
E-mail: orders@HeartsOnline.com
URL: www.HeartsOnline.com

ORDER FORM

I would like to order:

Putting Your Heart Online: Matchmaker Edition
Number of copies: _____ at $18.95 each _____

Sales Tax:

California residents add 8.25% sales tax _____
New Jersey residents add 6% sales tax _____

Shipping:

Within North America	free
Within the USA via Priority Mail	$3/book
Outside North America	$7/book
	Shipping _____

Payment Total _____

☐ Check enclosed in US dollars payable to Variable Symbols
☐ Credit card: ☐ AMEX ☐ MasterCard ☐ Visa
Card number: _____
Name on card: _____ Exp. date: __ /__
Signature: _____

Ship to:

Name: _____
Address: _____
_____
City: _____ State: _____
Zip: _____ Country: _____
Phone: _____ Fax: _____
E-mail: _____

E-mail or send orders to:

Variable Symbols, Inc.
33 Linda Avenue, Suite 2210
Oakland, CA 94611-4819
E-mail: orders@HeartsOnline.com
URL: www.HeartsOnline.com